SEX, VIOLENCE & POWER IN SPORTS

RETHINKING MASCULINITY

SEX, VIOLENCE & POWER IN SPORTS

RETHINKING MASCULINITY

Michael A. Messner, Ph.D.
& Donald F. Sabo, Ph.D.

The Crossing Press, Freedom, CA 95019

Photo Credits
S.U.N.Y. Buffalo Audio-Visual Center 13
Salinas High School El Gabilan 19
Fred A. Raab 28
CSU Hayward Pioneer 31, 36, 49, 66, 84, 85, 101, 106, 107, 131, 181, 193, 216, 217
Amy Sibiga 42, 161, 166, 167, 214
AP/Wide World Photos 59, 125, 157
Irene Fertik 174
Andrew Uchin 74 (artwork)
United Artists release 93

Interior design by Amy Sibiga
Printed in the U. S. A.

Library of Congress Cataloging-in-Publication Data

Messner, Michael A.
Sex, violence & power in sports : rethinking masculinity/ Michael A. Messner & Donald F. Sabo.
p. cm.
Includes bibliographical references.
ISBN 0-89594-689-0 (cloth). -- ISBN 0-89594-688-2 (paper)
1. Sports--Sociological aspects. 2. Sports--Psychological aspects. 3. Masculinity (psychology) 4. Violence in sports. 5. Gay athletes. 6. Power (Social sciences) I. Sabo, Donald F. II. Title. III. Title: Sex, violence and power in sports.
GV706.5.M47 1994
306.4'83--dc20 94-18562
CIP

ACKNOWLEDGMENTS

Since the stories and essays in this book were written over the course of many years, the people who have directly or indirectly influenced us are too many to list here. But we would like to express our gratitude to the women's movement and to the women's studies scholars who first explored and mapped out many of the gender questions and issues that we develop here. We also want to thank our friends and allies in the women's sports community whose work has inspired us: Deborah Slaner Anderson, Eva Auchencloss, Ellie Bulie, Phyllis Lerner, Donna Lopiano, Mariah Burton Nelson, Carole Oglesby, Katherine Reith, Major Synder, and the Women's Sports Foundation.

We have drawn strength and knowledge from the gay liberation and profeminist men's movements—particularly the National Organization for Men Against Sexism (NOMAS) and Changing Men Magazine (formerly M). We especially appreciate the superb editing work of Changing Men editors Michael Biernbaum and Rick Cote on the stories and essays that are reprinted here. For his never-failing vision and continued support, we warmly recognize our friend Michael Kimmel.

We are indebted to our colleagues in sport studies (especially those in the North American Society for the Sociology of Sport): Susan Birrell, Cheryl Cole, Margaret Carlisle Duncan, Mary Duquin, Stan Eitzen, Ann Hall, Bruce Kidd, Alan Klein, Richard Lapchick, Genevieve Rail, Earl Smith, Yevonne Smith, Nancy Theberge, and David Whitson. And we thank our wider circle of friends and colleagues who have encouraged and inspired us: Maxine Baca Zinn, Felix Baretto, Bob Blauner, Bob Connell, Bob Dunn, James Forman, Barry Glassner, Pat Griffen, Donnie Hallstone, Michel Hondagneu, Merrill Melnick, Peter Nardi, Ed Powell, Denise Roche, Barrie Thorne, and Jon Scattini. Special thanks to our old friends—and collaborators on two pieces in this book—Sue Curry Jansen and Bill Solomon. We appreciate the vision and skill of our editor at the Crossing Press, John Gill, in helping us to pull this work together into a book. Thanks also to Karen Narita and Amy Sibiga for their skillful and artistic production work.

Since the stories and essays in this book were written over the course of several years, it seems only fitting that we dedicate the book to the two women with whom each of us has lived and loved over those years. Pierrette Hondagneu-Sotelo has not only been Mike's spouse and colleague, she has also lovingly supported (or at least, at times, tolerated) his continued obsession with exploring hisown and other men's relationships to sports. And loving thanks to Linda Weisbeck Sabo, who, for nearly two decades, has worked to build the fulcrum upon which she and Don have balanced their lives and aspirations.

Introduction (Revised) by Mike Messner and Don Sabo (1991) "The Feminist Transformation of Sport," *Changing Men: Issues in Gender, Sex and Politics* 22 (Winter/Spring) pp. 50-52. I. Our Stories section introduction by Don Sabo (1980) "The Best Years of My Life," pp. 74-78 in D. F. Sabo and R. Runfola, eds. *Jock: Sports and Male Identity*. Mike Messner (1981) "Indignities: A Short Story," *M: Gentle Men for Gender Justice* 6 (Fall) pp. 12-13, 38-39. Mike Messner (1983/4) "Ah, Ya Throw Like a Girl!" *M: Gentle Men for Gender Justice* 11 (Winter) pp. 21-22. II. Sexuality and Power section introduction by Don Sabo (1989) "The Myth of the Sexual Athlete," *Changing Men: Issues in Gender, Sex and Politics* 20 pp. 38-39. Mike Messner (1991) "Women in the Men's Locker Room?" *Changing Men: Issues in Gender, Sex and Politics* 23 (Fall/Winter) pp. 56-58. Mike Messner and Bill Solomon (1992) "Sin and Redemption: The Sugar Ray Leonard Wife Abuse Story," *Changing Men: Issues in Gender, Sex and Politics* 25: 50-52, 54-55 (Revised). Mike Messner (1993) "Riding With the Spur Posse" *Changing Men: Issues in Gender, Sex and Politics* 27. III. Violence, Pain and Injury section introduction by Mike Messner (1983) "Why Rocky III?" *M: Gentle Men for Gender Justice* 10 (Spring) pp. 15-17. Don Sabo (1986) "Pigskin, Patriarchy, and Pain," *Changing Men: Issues in Gender, Sex and Politics* 16 pp. 24-25. Mike Messner (1990) "When Bodies Are Weapons," *Changing Men: Issues in Gender, Sex and Politics* 21. IV. Gay Athletes and Homophobia. Mike Messner (1984) "Gay Athletes and the Gay Games: An Interview with Tom Waddell," *M: Gentle Men for Gender Justice* 13 (Fall) pp. 22-23. Mike Messner (1993) "AIDS, Homophobia, and Sports," (A substantially new piece, containing a segment from the 1988 piece that appeared in *Changing Men: Issues in Gender, Sex and Politics* 19 pp. 30-32.) V. Marginal Men section introduction by Mike Messner (1986) "Sports and the Politics of Inequality," *Changing Men: Issues in Gender, Sex and Politics* 17 (Winter) pp. 27-28. Mike Messner (1993) "White Men Misbehaving: Feminism, Afrocentrism, and the Promise of a Critical Standpoint," *Journal of Sport and Social Issues* 16 pp. 136-144, (Revised). Don Sabo & Sue Curry Jansen (1993) "Seen But Not Heard: Black Men in Sports Media," *Changing Men: Issues in Gender, Sex and Politics* 26 (Summer/Fall) pp. 46-49. VI. Changing Sports, Changing Men section introduction by Don Sabo (1980) "Getting Beyond Exercise as Work," pp. 290-299 in D. F. Sabo and R. Runfola, eds. *Jock: Sports and Male Identity*. Mike Messner (1985) "Jocks in the Men's Movement?" *Changing Men: Issues in Gender, Sex and Politics* 14 (Spring) pp. 34-35. Don Sabo (1993) "Feminist Analysis of Men in Sports," (Revised version of 1987 piece that appeared in *Changing Men: Issues in Gender, Sex and Politics* 18 pp. 31-32.) Mike Messner (1987) "Boys and Girls Together: The Promise and Limits of Equal Opportunity," *Equal Play* (Fall) pp. 18-19.

For

Pierrette Hondagneu-Sotelo

and

Linda Weisbeck Sabo

CONTENTS

CONTENTS

FOREWORD

You are about to read a very personal book by two sportsmen who are willing to share their intimacies about being male and being athletes. You may be shocked by the violent and insensitive reality of the locker room we have created for our sons. You will doubt whether sport is a positive learning experience. You will ask whether our current model of American sport reinforces and perpetuates social injustice and individual oppression. At the very least, you will rethink the male sport experience in our country and how it relates to violence (especially violence against women), the athlete's inability to express intimacy, and the perpetuation of gender, class and racial inequality and homophobia.

Messner and Sabo address our worst fears about male athletes. Are they more likely to be rapists? Are they celebrated for their sexual conquests and protected by the boys' club of the mass media? Are they incapable of engaging in relationships that don't have winners and losers? Have they been so brainwashed by coaches that they ignore physical pain and permanent injury in the name of upholding the image of macho athletes? Do they so dehumanize their opponents that violence and intentional maiming are accomplished with joy rather than guilt? Are they so intimidated by the prospect of rejection by their peers through accusations of homosexuality or feminization that they can no longer make ethical decisions about their actions? The answers to these questions should worry each of us.

Fortunately, Messner and Sabo are not satisfied with just being analysts and critics. They are passionate believers that sports participation can be an exhilarating, rewarding, and positive experience. So, they have given us "their best shots" regarding how we can change the sport experience for men and encourage women not to follow the male model. They show us that there are ways to recreate sport for men and women so the positive possibilities can be realized: that opponents can be friends engaged in a mutual test rather than being enemies to be defeated; that the effort to win is as important as winning; that the spirit of sport is as important as its rules; that intentionally causing injury to another is totally unacceptable; that men and women can play with and against each other without questioning their sexual preference or to whom the fields of sport belong.

This book is the right stuff for the television and radio talk show circuit. The ideas presented here deserve popular and critical academic review. It will be interesting to see if the male sport culture and those who support it are willing to take a close and unbecoming look at themselves.

Donna Lopiano, Ph.D.
Executive Director
Women's Sports Foundation
East Meadow, New York

Introduction

MIKE MESSNER AND DON SABO

The stories and essays in this book are part of an effort to change the patriarchal status quo and, with feminist theory, to forge new understandings of the old relationship between men and sports. Sports are central to many men's lives, and even men who don't like to play or follow sports are affected by them. Hence, feminist-inspired reflection on the personal and political dimensions of sports can give us insights into ourselves and the larger system of gender relations.

As boys, we were initiated into the world of sports by men and into the world of men through sports. For both of us, sports have had a joyous upside and a very limiting, often painful downside. Mike has always known an existential high in shooting a basketball through a hoop. From an early age he found that sports participation was the key to his relationship with his father and eventually with his peers. But as he passed through adolescence into adulthood he became increasingly aware of how the athletic role, with its narrow definition of success and failure, limited the foundation upon which his self-image was constructed. Though sports formed a basis for relationships with some males, he also became aware of how the competition, homophobia, and misogyny in the sports world limited his ability to develop intimate relationships with women and other men.

Like Mike's, Don's athletic experiences have shifted between joy and misery, healthful release and personal harm. Having discovered football as a fourth grader in western Pennsylvania, he went on to play and love the game throughout his college years. Football was a way to make friendships and build self-confidence. Ultimately it became a ticket out of the steel mills and into a university. The patriarchal piper demanded his pay, however, and the hypermasculine, physically brutal aspects of the game took their toll. Six years of chronic back pain and surgery prompted Don to rethink the beliefs and practices that informed his involvement in traditional men's sports.

GETTING OUR FEMINIST VISION

Our critical perception of sports took many years to develop. Change flowed slowly; we did not wake up one day and see sports in utterly new ways. Our most crucial source of critical illumination was the women's movement of the late 1960s and 1970s. Feminist women created new frameworks of meaning through which we could examine our experiences. Had the women's movement and feminist theory not developed in the seventies, we are certain that we, as men and as former athletes, would not be examining the masculinity-sports relationship. To do so would never have crossed our minds.

At first we each questioned and struggled alone. Few men embraced feminist vision in the early seventies. There were books, conferences, and consciousness-raising groups for women, but not many liberative resources explicitly for men. The few men who publicly declared their commitment to feminism usually faced justifiable caution from women and blank stares or jeers from other men. Among the few profeminist men we knew, discussions of sports were usually limited to hasty condemnations. Many of these men had, as boys, been hurt—physically and emotionally—by their inability or unwillingness to "measure up" in Little League baseball or other competitive sports organized by men for boys. Their dismissal of sports was understandable, and we profeminist jocks, feeling somewhat guilty about our continued ambivalence about sports, entered into a tacit agreement not to discuss them. The unwillingness to talk about an activity that was so important to us contributed to our feelings of isolation in profeminist groups and organizations.

Liberation is a road seldom traveled alone, and our personal and scholarly investigations of sports and gender took a quantum leap forward when we discovered each other's ideas. While Mike had been writing about men's lives in sports on the West Coast, Don was researching men and masculinity on the East Coast. We met through a 1982 book review that Mike wrote of Don's and Ross Runfola's book *Jock: Sports and Male Identity*. We wrote to each other, and when we realized that we had similar political views, our friendship quickly deepened, along with our analysis of sports, masculinity, and sexism. We helped each other locate other profeminists who shared our analytical obsession with sports and gender. In the process we constructed a network of soul mates. In short, our personal and intellectual quest took nurture from—and at the same time contributed to—a growing array of progressive social movements, ideas, and political networks. We want to discuss some of these larger historical processes as we now see them.

FEMINIST VIEWS OF SPORTS

The feminist analysis of sports has a very short history. Before the 1980s, sex and gender issues in sports were hardly mentioned in mainstream feminist literature. Simone de Beauvoir's *The Second Sex* (1952), Kate Millett's *Sexual Politics* (1971), Juliet Mitchell's *Women's Estate* (1973), Susan Brownmiller's *Against Our Will* (1975), Mary Daly's *GynEcology: The Metaethics of Radical Feminism* (1978), and Betty Friedan's *The Second Stage* (1981) all lack any substantive treatment of sports.

Despite the lack of attention the wider women's movement gave to sports, by the late seventies feminists in academia began to develop a critique of sports as a fundamentally male-dominated, sexist institution. Feminist analyses uncovered the hidden history of female athletics, examined sex differences in patterns of athletic socialization, and showed how dominant institutional forms of sport have made men's power and privilege over women seem natural. Sports, especially as they are presented by the mass media, help to uphold an otherwise faltering ideology of male superiority. The language of sports is the language of domination, and it permeates the nation's discourse in politics, education, and the boardroom.

MEN'S STUDIES OF SPORT

During the 1960s most men were only vaguely aware that important connections exist between themselves, sports, and inequality. In keeping with the mainly masculine agenda of the New Left, emerging critical commentary on sports and sexism was superficially subsumed into radical rhetoric on class and race inequality.

The earliest feminist critiques of sports and patriarchy in the 1970s led some men to reflect on their relationships to sports. A number of radical critics of sports included some treatment of gender issues in their overall class or racial analyses. Paul Hoch (1972) labeled sports a "school for sexism;" Mark Naison (1972) saw sports as an institutional source of the "ideology of male domination." The writings of Jack Scott (1971) and Harry Edwards (1973) not only unraveled the links between sports ideology, class relations, and race inequality, but they also discussed sex segregation and inequality in sports. Other writers, inspired by the mid-1970s "men's liberation movement," contributed to the discussion. Warren Farrell (1974), Marc Fasteau (1974), and Robert Townshend (1977) focused on the cultural significance of sports and the emotional harm caused by athletic training for aggression and extreme competitiveness.

Sabo and Runfola's 1980 book *Jock*, a consciously profeminist analysis of sports, attempted to prompt men to understand themselves as individual victims of sexual inequality without losing sight of the fact that they are the collective oppressors of women. This represented a departure from the analyses presented both by the radical critics, who tended to collapse gender issues into a race or class dynamic, and by men's liberationists, who tended to focus on how narrow definitions of masculinity hurt men while downplaying or ignoring how sports help establish and legitimate male privilege.

During the 1980s, feminists recognized the need for the development of a more relational theory of gender, one that would include a critical examination of both femininity and masculinity, as they develop in relation to each other within a system of structured social inequality. Recently, feminist scholarship has germinated what some are calling a "new men's studies." Men's studies scholars see in feminism a perspective that holds the potential of liberating men as well as women from the limitations of sexism.

The feminist vision of sports and gender came of age in the 1980s. Male analysts openly expressed their debt to the feminist paradigm. Theories became more exact and lucid, research mushroomed, and the subfield of "Sport and Gender Studies" became grafted to the intellectual and political agenda of women's studies and men's studies. Though still on the margins of mainline social science, the gender issue in sports could no longer be denied. Women and men dialogued and collaborated with one another, and an international network of individuals struggling for gender justice in athletics took shape.

In the midst of these developments, between 1980 and 1994, we wrote the stories and essays that appear in this book. Fifteen of the twenty-four works in this book were originally published in *Changing Men* (originally *M*) magazine; four were previously published elsewhere; and five are original works, written for this book. Ranging from personal stories from our own athletic careers to political commentary on contemporary athletic controversies and research on current issues in sports, this collection illustrates the feminist observation that our personal experiences often reflect much larger social and political patterns. We offer this collection not only as a reflection on our own experiences as jocks, but as a contribution to a clearer understanding of men's relationship with sports, in the hope that women, men, and sports will change in more humane and egalitarian directions.

For more than a century, feminists have challenged us to look critically at gender issues and eliminate some of the injustices that attend sex inequality. Feminists have often indicted men for their sexist behavior and chauvinistic attitudes. Some men have reacted defensively to these charges; some have gotten angry; many have been confused. Others, though, have been able to hear women's angry protests, political and cultural dreams, and messages from the heart, and have viewed feminism as an opportunity to rethink and remake their personal, sexual, and social lives. Especially in recent years, some men have begun to think about, feel about, and talk about themselves in new ways.

We men who think of ourselves as profeminists have learned that feminist visions and values can help us make our way through life. We seek not only to end sexist oppression of women, but also, along with other men, to change some of the destructive aspects of our own lives and identities. We are convinced that feminist perspectives on sports can help men to rethink and redefine manhood and society in ways that bolster rather than erode our capabilities to love and to survive.

Today much of the athletic experience is distorted or muted by sexism, homophobia, and aggressive domination thinly disguised as "healthy competition." The life-affirming dimensions of sports, however, are waiting to be drawn forth and nurtured. A feminist transformation of sports can help us realize this potential.

REFERENCES

Edwards, Harry, 1973. *Sociology of Sport*. Homewood, IL: Dorsey.

Farrell, Warren, 1974. *The Liberated Man*. New York: Bantam.

Fasteau, Marc-Feigan, 1974. *The Male Machine*. New York: McGraw-Hill.

Hoch, Paul, 1972. *Rip Off the Big Game*. New York: Doubleday.

Naison, Mark, 1972. "Sports, Women and the Ideology of Domination." *Radical America* (July-August) p. 95.

Sabo, Donald F. and Ross Runfola, eds., 1977. *Jock: Sports and Male Identity*. Englewood Cliffs, NJ: Prentice-Hall.

Scott, Jack, 1971. *The Athletic Revolution*. London: The Free Press.

Townsend, Robert C., 1977. "The Competitive Male as Loser." pp. 266-79 in Donald F. Sabo and Ross Runfola, eds., *Jock: Sports and Male Identity*. Englewood Cliffs, NJ: Prentice-Hall.

Part I

OUR STORIES

As boys, we loved sports. We *lived* sports. In the pre-cable TV era in which we grew up, our favorite television show was "The Wide World of Sports." The opening of the show is indelibly etched in our memories: An enthusiastic and authoritative male announcer invites the viewers to share in "the thrill of victory and the agony of defeat," as a rapid succession of images of male athletes at glorious pinnacles of their careers (George Forman throwing kisses to a frenzied crowd, for instance, after seizing the heavyweight championship of the world) are counterposed with images of spectacular failures (a skier crashing and plunging off the end of the ski jump).

As boys eager to become men, we wanted to experience the "thrill of victory" ourselves, and to share in the glory and public adulation enjoyed by our heroes, Willie Mays, Jim Ryun, Oscar Robertson, Dick Butkus, and Big Daddy Liscomb. But we were also well aware of the other side of sports. One athlete's thrilling victory is inevitably another's agonizing defeat. One champion's glorious moment is another's moment of loss, even humiliation. One famous athlete's storied career is another's attempt fallen short. But there were always ready explanations for the failed jock: Perhaps he didn't practice hard enough. Perhaps he "had a bad attitude." Perhaps he just wasn't good enough.

We practiced hard. We had the attitude that our coaches loved. And yet our athletic accomplishments usually fell far short of our dreams. Perhaps, we had to finally admit to ourselves, we just weren't good enough. Oh, we each had a few fleeting moments of glory, moments in which years of practicing and visualizing success translated for Mike into a perfect give-and-go play with a basketball teammate, or for Don a perfect defensive read and solo tackle on the gridiron. But given the growing prevalence of the Lombardian Ethic, the belief that "winning is everything," we often experienced even our most modest athletic accomplishments as dismal failures.

The fact that we both experienced more agony than ecstasy in doing what we loved most, playing sports, made us feel as though something was seriously deficient or wrong with us as individuals. Many years after the ends of our athletic careers, we learned from feminist women to examine our personal experiences and problems within the context of larger social realities. The idea that "the personal is political" allowed us to see our own bad experiences in sports not as manifestations of personal failure, but as normal consequences in a system that values victory over all else, including relationships with others and even one's own health. The stories in this section represent our efforts to reexamine, through a feminist lens, some of our youthful experiences as athletes. We offer this critical look at our jock experiences largely because, after all these years, we still passionately love sports. And, as subsequent sections of the book will show, we believe that sports can be changed so all players can experience some of the ecstasy that too often is lost in modern sport.

The Best Years of My Life

DON SABO

What is it like becoming a football player? In my case, the process began in 1955, when I was eight years old. At the time—and this feeling still takes possession of me—I felt uncomfortable inside my body. Too fat, too short, too weak. Freckles and glasses, too! I wanted to change my image, and changing my body was the place to begin. My parents bought me a set of weights, and asked one of the older boys in the neighborhood to demonstrate their use. I can still remember the ease with which he lifted the barbell, the veins popping through his bulging biceps in the summer sun, and the sated look of strength and accomplishment on his face. This image was to be my future.

That fall I made a dinner-table announcement that I was going out for football. The initiation rites were inauspicious. My flesh was pricked with thorns until blood flowed, and hot peppers were rubbed into my eyes. I was forced to wear a jockstrap around my nose, and I didn't know what was funny. Then came what was to be an endless series of ways of proving myself. Calisthenics until my arms ached. Hitting hard and fast and knocking the other guy down. Getting hit in the groin and not crying. Striving to be a leader. Ten thousand Hail Marys later, having reveled in moments of glory and endured hours of shame, my grade school football days were over. The post-season banquet was like all the others. The men made speeches and the women cooked and served dinner.

By the time I reported for my first high-school practice as a "Crimson Crusher," I already knew what was expected of me. The object was to beat out the other guy. I already had it in my head that the way to succeed was to be an animal. Coaches took notice of animals. Animals made the first team. Being an animal meant being ruthlessly aggressive and competitive. If you saw an arm in front of you, you trampled it. Whenever blood was spilled, you nodded approval. It's no wonder that, of all the friendships I formed in those years, only two survive—one with a married country-club manager in my hometown, and the other with a hippie silversmith in California. Friendships with other males were always tempered by competition. A friend today could rob you of your position tomorrow. The idea was to slap backs, but not get too close emotionally.

As for friendships with women, they were virtually impossible. All that boys and girls were supposed to do together were neck and pet, and the cheerleaders were the most sought-after girls. On the sidelines and in the stands the boys, and probably the men, watched the girls' breasts bounce and waited for cartwheels.

I was eventually elected captain of the football team, had a good senior year, and hoped and prayed for a college scholarship. In Johnstown, Pennsylvania, in 1965, a football scholarship meant going to college and not to the steel mills. The mills were the alternative that pounded my adolescent eardrums. I was recruited by several schools—going the round of dates, drunks, and interviews with star athletes and coaches. I felt important but, beneath it all, damned insecure and afraid.

By this time, my body had undergone a thorough metamorphosis. My hair was short, and my biceps were eighteen inches around. My

Don Sabo (circa 1968) hoped to escape working in the steel mills by becoming a ruthlessly competitive and aggressive competitor on the gridiron.

chest, which I measured periodically, pressed through tight T-shirts. I held my belly in, especially when women were nearby. The tenderness and sensitivity that lay scrunched inside me were carefully hidden. I felt like I was living inside a tank. The structure was formidably protective, but oppressively rigid.

College football was both a joy and affliction. I felt great running for hours without tiring, responding with nimble alacrity when split-second reactions were required, drinking in those sweet moments in which body and mind worked as one. But then there were the broken noses, fingers, toes, and teeth; torn muscles, bruises, bad knees, and busted lips; and the back problems that are with me to this day. Parents, fans, and supportive teachers or administrators were always there with congratulations and encouragement. Though I didn't realize it then, I know now that their approval stemmed from the fact that I was verifying a way of life they held sacred.When we ballplayers, clad in fiberglass armor, made our triumphant entrance into the stadium, they would cheer and feel that their values were still intact. America was still the beautiful. Young men still struggled against one another. Competition reigned supreme. As for myself, I always held "the fans" in contempt. They worshipped a game they knew little about. I can still hear their high-pitched voices yelling "Kill 'em, Sabo!"

Perhaps the saddest thing that happened in college was that the game became a job. Just being an animal didn't work anymore. Technical expertise was the new goal. As the coaches put it, "You have to make sure your body is in the right place at the right time." Game plans were devised, studied, and executed as assiduously as corporate annual reports. Coaches monitored our movements on and off the field. No staying out late. No bars. No long hair. No marijuana. No lovemaking during forty-eight hours before a game. No involvement in New Left politics because this didn't fit the all-American boy image. The coaches even told us what to say to the press. What we felt or thought didn't matter. Good public relations meant big box office sales. Bad injuries meant ostracism, obsolescence, and in some cases no more scholarship, but as long as your body functioned well on the field, coaches and alumni were "behind you." We were flattered and paid to "do the job."

We played not for our own pleasure but for that of others, and talk about team spirit was publicity hype for the fans. Very often, I felt as if I had ended up in the steel mills after all.

Elected captain in my senior year, I played "the last game" at Boston University. When the final whistle blew, I dropped my helmet on the sidelines and burst into tears. They weren't tears of joy. I cried out of a sense of release—from a form of bondage I didn't yet understand. I vowed never to allow anyone to treat me as a jock again. I dieted and lost forty pounds, kept to myself, and began to make friends in the counterculture. Five years passed before I could bring myself to do something competitive—play a game of checkers with an eight-year-old boy.

My father often tells me, smiling gently, that my college years were the best years of my life, that I would live them over again if I could. I always reply, "No. I'd do something else." He never quite believes me. To be honest, I'm not sure I believe myself. In the hearts of many boys and men, the image of themselves as star athletes burns brightly. The stars' world is a "promised land"—full of notoriety, women, sex, and status. I walked in its gardens and tasted its fruits. The fruits were sour. However, had I never "made it" in athletics, I wouldn't be the same person today. I might still be chasing the kind of masculine ideal athletic success held out to me. It feels good to be out of the race.

Author's note: The inspiration for this essay came from Michael Eugene Luzny, former teammate and current friend.

Indignities: A Short Story

MIKE MESSNER

So here we were at the state tournament. Coach Milton had told us from the start that we would make it. We won our conference, and then our region, and all with nobody on the team over six-foot-three. I was proud to be a part of the team, sitting here in the bleachers together joking around as we watched the opening game of the tournament and awaited our opener later that night.

Sure, I had hardly gotten to play in any of our games all season long—and, when I had, it was either after victory had been safely tucked away for the old alma mater, or when we had been hopelessly blown away by the opponent. But I'd had my moment of glory. Early in the season I had gotten into a game for the last two minutes. We were leading by about thirty points and the first and second string had long since sat down and left the mop-up work for the hack squad. With just a few seconds left, I got the ball to the right side of the free throw line and threw in a jump shot. I was pleased, but not elated. I had scored my share of points as a high school player, and in situations where it really mattered, and I felt that I could do so in college as well. But as the season wore on, I played in fewer and fewer games—none of which allowed me the opportunity to get up my second shot of the season. I began to realize that I had a record to protect. I was one-for-one. That's a very impressive 1.000 shooting percentage, and good enough for the national leadership. So I began to pass up shots when the opportunity presented itself. Although the mass media ignored this fact, I was for most of the 1970 to 1971 season the national leader in shooting percentage in the Community College Division of basketball.

But this was the state tournament, and all that was past. Rex, our top rebounder, was sitting below me looking at his program, and he turned back and said to me, "Hey, Mess—what's this about you being the team manager?"

I didn't know what he was talking about. "What? Let me see that thing." And there it was, in black and white—I was listed in the tournament program not as a player, but as the team manager. Team manager. A job that includes supplying towels during time-outs, as well as taking plenty of verbal abuse from players. Indeed, in the past I had never had much to do with managers of teams I had played on. Managers were guys who liked sports but couldn't play, so they tagged along with the big boys and did all the shit work. We called them "jock sniffers." I was pissed.

I spotted Coach Milton sitting on the opposite side of the gym, surveying the action with some fellow coaches. As I briskly walked across the gym towards him, memories swirled through my head: Milton telling me early in the season that I was going to "play a lot of ball"; being the only player on the team who didn't get to play in a game which we won by 25 points; Milton's pumping up the basketball with too much air so it would take longer rebounds and give us an edge over a team of very tall players. He was an opportunist, a manipulator of situations and people who used his own players as means toward his personal ends of winning—winning basketball games and championships, which he saw as his keys to eventually moving up into the major college coaching ranks.

Taking the bleacher steps two at a time, with no prepared speech, I finally faced Milton. "What's this all about?" I demanded as I thrust the program onto his lap. "What's this 'manager' stuff?"

Milton could see that I was upset. "Oh, yeah, Mike. I forgot to tell you about that. The tournament rules state that we can have only twelve players suited up and we have thirteen. The only way I could bring you along was to list you as the manager."

"You were doing me a favor? Do you realize how fucking embarrassing this is?"

He was not too pleased with my manner, especially since his fellow coaches were listening. "Get the hell back to the motel, and pack your bags. None of my players talk to me like that!" Presumably, none of his managers could talk to him like that either. I wanted to yell and scream about what I felt was a gross injustice, but justice took a back seat to a more immediate problem—I was losing my self-control. Tears were welling up in my eyes and my face felt like a Solarcaine commercial. I knew that all the guys were watching us from across the gym, so I retired to the nearest restroom to get myself under control.

When I came out of the restroom, still shaken, I was met by my buddy Robby T., with whom I had shared the end of the bench all season. He gave me a tentative smile. "You okay?"

Deflated, I didn't want to talk much. "Yeah," I managed. "I'd like to get out of here."

"Let's go," Robby T. said.

As we walked back toward the motel, we didn't say much. We threw rocks into a shallow creek and silently walked into a crisp March evening.

My demotion to "jock sniffer" was the culmination of a tumultuous year for me. The season of 1970 to 1971 was a painful year—a year of indignities, a year in which I found that the ways that I had always measured myself against others (mostly through basketball) no longer worked for me. As I failed in the old ways, I searched for new ways to "measure up." Very little worked out very well.

Mike Messner (circa 1970) was a better-than-average high school basketball player but in college he found that he was too short to play forward, too slow to play guard, so he was demoted to "jock sniffer."

Early in the season, we played a practice game against the freshman team at the University of Santa Clara. Two of our starters got a bit drunk on the trip up to Santa Clara. I kept worrying that the coach or the referees would smell the booze. (A few weeks earlier, a guy had been kicked off our team for coming to practice drunk—after Milton had sniffed around like a bloodhound for an hour to determine who the guilty party was.) One of the two drinkers got kicked out of the game early for fighting, and the other fouled out early in the second half.

For me, however, the main significance of this game was that we lost 100 to 51, which meant that I got to play during the last three minutes of the game. This was hack-squad time—all the pent-up frustration of bench-time released in three or four minutes of frantic action. Since the referees just wanted time to run out, they wouldn't blow their whistles if a freight train came thundering down the center of the gym. Which isn't too far from what actually happened.

As time ran down, Robby T. was under the hoop with the ball. He went up with it and was clobbered by an opponent. No whistle blew. He went up with a second shot and was hacked from three sides. Still no whistle. As he went up with the ball for a third time, several things happened simultaneously: the buzzer went off; the referees retreated quickly and quietly to the safety of their dressing room; and Robby T. came down swinging. He and Mitch soon had some poor slob up against the wall, and they were pounding away at his stomach. Drew flew off the bench and hit the first Santa Clara player he could reach with an uppercut to the jaw that lifted the guy off his feet and left him on his back on the floor.

I was dead-center in the middle of it all and quite concerned for my health. Actually, I was scared shitless. I turned to watch as the opponents' bench emptied onto the floor toward us—toward me! Two huge brutes ran directly at me—like Greek gods, they were each about six-five and quite muscular. I knew I would soon be hit, so I did the only thing I could under the circumstances—I disappeared. Or so it seemed, for the two Greek gods on a mission to massacre me simply ran right by, one on either side, nearly brushing my shoulders.

Now confidently protected by my invisibility, I turned to watch the action. Coach Milton had a Santa Clara player in a half-nelson as Pete pummeled the kid's midsection. An older Santa Clara fan was screaming at Milton, "Get your goddamned junior college team off the floor!"

"Fuck you, just fuck you," blurted back a seething Milton.

A few minutes later, in the safety of the locker room, there was silence as Coach Milton entered the room, red-faced. "Did everybody get a good one in?" he asked us in a shout.

"Yeah!" was the unanimous response.

"Good," snorted Milton. "If we can't kick their asses in one way, we'll kick their asses in another way." He seemed satisfied.

Now it was clearly face-saving time for those who didn't "get a good one in." Pete asked me, "Hey, Mess, I didn't see you out there—were you there?"

"Hell, yes," I replied. "I was right in the center of all the action."

Several of the guys seemed peeved at Kess. "Kess didn't do *nothin'*. He just stood by the bench and watched. Some teammate, Kess."

Kess just shook his head. He was, in addition to being a pretty nifty ball-handler, a concert pianist. He clearly didn't want to risk injuring his hands in a brawl that resulted from a 100 to 51 loss.For the rest of the season, Kess was an outsider. He rarely got to play in games any more. When I roomed with Kess a few weeks later on a road trip, I took a lot of ribbing for it from the other guys. Word had it now that Kess was a "fag." "Hey, Mess, you having fun with Kess in that room at night?" they'd laugh. "Don't Mess with Kess," they would sing. I liked Kess, but I avoided him after that. It was bad enough being the lowest player on the team totem pole; the last thing I needed was to be thought a fag.

As each weekend neared, the coach would invariably treat us to a grueling practice session followed by a speech in which he warned us of the evils of "dissipation." "Remember to stay away from the booze and split-tails," he would admonish us. He knew as well as we did that drinking and the pursuit of sex were all part of a basketball player's lifestyle, but he did his duty in warning us of the dangers of such activities.

On one road trip, while five or six of us were in a motel room having a few beers, the subject of sex came up. Robby T. and I kept our mouths shut and listened intently as Drew and Sal debated the ins and outs of "eating pussy." Sal was adamant: "Man, I'd *never* do that."

But Drew was calm and convincing. Unlike Robby T. and me, who had led the sheltered lives of white middle-class kids in a small town, Drew was a somewhat older, experienced (or so he had us convinced) black guy from a Brooklyn ghetto. He knew the street—crime, drugs, fights—and he knew about eating pussy. "Hey man," he said to Sal and to the rest of us, "it can be the sweetest thing a man can do. They love it, man. You gotta try it."

"Not me, man." Sal was unmoved by Drew's testimony. He made a face that suggested a permanent bad taste in his mouth.

Finally, I suppose, they noticed that Robby T. and I had been silent all through the conversation. We were still virgins, slowly progressing up the erotic ladder with our respective girlfriends. We kept silent so as not to betray our ignorance and lack of experience. Drew asked, "Hey, Robby T., hey, Mess, you guys ever had a piece of ass?"

I knew how to play this game. Everyone knew that I had a girlfriend, and so long as I didn't talk about it, but just gave a sly smile every time the subject came up, people would assume that I was getting laid.

"What about it, Mess, you gettin' any?"

"Naw," I replied, with diverted eyes and a knowing smile on my face. Robby T. seemed to like this strategy, too, so he followed suit. But damned if Drew didn't take us literally—he totally missed the subtle, calculated smile intended to communicate that "yes, of course I can get some ass anytime I like, but I'm far too much of a gentleman to talk about my sex life with my girlfriend around other people."

"Wow!" exclaimed Drew, "We got two virgins on this team! We can't have that! Mess, Robby T., we gotta get you laid, and soon. We can't go havin' any virgins on this team. Havin' Kess is bad enough!" Robby T. and I were bewildered.

A couple of weeks later, Drew invited us to a party. Robby T. and I showed up with our usual case of Olympia beer. Oly was our brand because of the labels on the bottles. When you ripped off the label, you'd find imprinted on the reverse side one, two, three, or four dots. Legend had it that if a guy could get a woman to sign her name on his label, he could by right claim some booty—a hug for one dot, a kiss for two, or a feel for three. Four was the grand slam. We coveted those rare "fours" and even carried them in our wallets, "just in case."

This night at Drew's house, Robby T. had just gotten a "four," and we were joking about who he should get to sign it. Drew broke in on us and said, "Hey, you two virgins ain't gonna be virgins after tonight, eh?"

We thought he was referring to the Oly labels, so we agreed with him and laughed. "Sure, Drew. We're just trying to figure out who we want to lay tonight."

"Man, you don't have to worry about that, because me and the guys have that taken care of. We got a lady comin' over here in a couple of hours. She's real special, an' since you guys are the only two virgins on the team, you get to go first."

I could feel myself tense up, but I knew that I was supposed to act grateful. "Wow, Drew. Like, is she some kind of prostitute or something?"

"You could say that," smiled Drew. "She's kind of a friend of mine, you know?" Drew laughed loud and hard, and so did we. I took some long pulls on my Oly, drained it, and opened another one. I whispered to Robby T., "Let's get the hell out of here."

Rob was feeling the same way I was, so we split out the back door with our Oly bottles under our arms and our unsigned "fours" in our wallets. We felt a bit ashamed at ourselves, but we decided that the only way to handle the guys when we next saw them was to tell them a lie: We were now laying our girlfriends and just couldn't do it with someone else because we wanted to be faithful. That's how we escaped being put on the "fag bag" with Kess. We were accepted now. We had learned how to bullshit about sex with the best of them.

One of the reasons that a coach keeps more guys on the team than he can possibly use is to have plenty of bodies around to play shit roles in practice. You get to play "dummy defense" so the *real* players can practice their plays and build their confidence without a struggle. You don't think. You don't try to steal the ball, block a shot, or anything.

After an hour or two of dummy defense, Milton would sometimes have us run a full-court "three-on-two drill." In this drill three players run the full length of the court dribbling and passing the ball towards two players, who try to stop them from scoring. As soon as someone scores, or as soon as the defense succeeds in stopping the offense, three more men head down the court. Mitch and I were the two defensive men.

Mitch was a tough cookie. A year older than I, he had been a great high school athlete. (The first shot that I ever took in a high-school varsity game was blocked by Mitch.) When he graduated from high school, the U.S. Marines told him he could pitch for their baseball team. He joined up, and found himself in Vietnam, where he became a hero by fielding a grenade instead of a ball and losing several fingers on both hands. There was no more baseball after that for Mitch, but, miraculously, he could still play pretty good basketball. He still shot right-handed, even though all he had on that side was his thumb and forefinger. He had a nice touch with that finger.

So Mitch and I would stand there, sometimes tandem, sometimes side by side, as threesome after threesome would attack us. We would try different strategies—feinting, faking, trying to disrupt their rhythm, or at least making them settle for a fifteen-foot shot rather than giving them a lay-up. Usually they scored, but sometimes we stopped them. One day, however, we got so inspired we were stopping them far more often than they were scoring—we were making steals, blocking shots, forcing them into mistakes. Mitch and I talked, jived, slapped hands. We had bonded together in one of those transcendent moments in sports where you just know what your teammate is going to do, and everything you do works. We felt like *basketball players* again.

At the end of practice, Milton announced that this had been the worst practice we had had in a long time—that the team had been flat and lackluster, and that we couldn't ever hope to beat anybody with such a performance. He made the whole team run extra laps before going in to shower.

"For that kind of effort, I want you sucking air through your assholes," he screamed at us as we ran and ran. "You may hate me now for this, but when you get into a game situation, nobody you face will ever be in better shape than you."

Me get into a game situation? Back to dummy defense.

As the final game of our regular season approached, my optimism was rekindled. Though I hadn't played in a game for several weeks, I, like most reserves, still had my fantasies about "getting my big chance." I had long since realized that my getting into a game that was not already clearly won or lost—getting in, that is, when it really mattered—would have taken a highly unlikely combination of sicknesses, injuries, and disqualifications among my teammates, or a moment of temporary insanity on the part of the coach. Neither of these things happened, so I sat and waited for those rare 25 to 30-point leads or deficits and my two or three minutes of play.

For the final couple of weeks, I placed my hopes for a chance to play in our final contest. Having locked up the conference championship, we were scheduled to play the last-place team on our home court. From Milton's point of view, this game would be just a tune-up for the regional playoffs. I knew I'd get a chance to play in this one, and I hoped I could perform well enough to make something from what had been otherwise a pretty dismal season for me.

I sat and watched, seemingly forever, as our starters, playing sluggishly, took most of the game to rack up a comfortable lead. When I finally got into the game, about four minutes were left, and I had an entire season's worth of energy in me. The guys had been encouraging me all week to take a few shots if I got the chance, so once I entered the game, they were working hard to set me up for some shots in front of the full-capacity crowd.

The first time down the court with the ball, we ran a play that freed me on the left side along the baseline. Kess threaded a perfect bounce-pass to me, and with no hesitation I fired up a fifteen-foot shot. It went only fourteen feet. Airball.

There was too much action and excitement to mourn my first miss of the season. I just dismissed it as my warm-up shot. The next time down the court, Robby T. set a perfect screen for me. As I came around the screen, Mitch made a crisp chest-pass to me. I found myself wide open with the ball just above the free-throw line, and suddenly I became aware of the crowd—urging me, yelling to me, commanding me, "SHOOOOT! SHOOOOT!" As I fired away, I could feel my arm stiffen, and the ball again found nothing but air.

The crowd was having a good time. Their team was winning handily and on its way to the regional playoffs. The hack squad was in mopping up, and the team clown was giving them some last thrills and spills. The only problem was that I didn't want that role. I was a basketball player, not a clown, and I knew it. But by now there was nothing I could do but play out the role. The script was written, and everyone knew their parts. The next opportunity I had, I threw a twenty-footer up and swished it. The crowd roared its approval. My teammates slapped me on the back. I hated it. I felt like shit.

How hard I tried to "measure up" that year. I spent money I didn't have on a stereo receiver that had more power (30 watts per channel) than any of my friends' stereos had—only to have a friend a few weeks later buy a 100-watt stereo. I compulsively drank beer after beer at parties, keeping count to be sure that nobody drank more than I—only to end up hugging a toilet afterward. I read *The Sensuous Man* and laid a ruler next to my penis, hoping that I was "above average"—only to find that I wasn't. And then I had to end my career in organized basketball by making a fool of myself, blowing my national shooting percentage title with two airballs, and finally being demoted to the lowly position of manager.

One might think that my demise as a basketball star would have taught me something about competition, about success. As my father used to tell me, "Sports is life—learn from it and you will do well in life." This story would have a relatively happy ending if I said I learned that the sports pyramid I so conscientiously climbed is rigged to bring about the total failure of everyone on it: the higher one climbs up the pyramid, the farther down one must fall when one is finally, and inevitably, pushed off by bigger, better, younger players.

But the story does not end in 1971. Or in 1980. The young man of 1971 simply found a new pyramid to climb. Whereas some climb the pyramid of "success" (work and consumption), I took on the pyramid of academe, where I am still confronted with a world which encourages me to forge people's names on the backs of beer labels. As a twenty-eight-year-old man, I am coming to see academe and sports as the same pyramid. The same ego game.

Yet, Lord, how I strive.

Ah, Ya Throw Like a Girl!

MIKE MESSNER

Although the sociology department at the University of California, Berkeley, is situated on the fourth floor of a very ugly postwar building, the place does have one thing going for it: the fourth-floor balcony overlooks the women's softball field. There I have spent more than a few fine afternoons in the past few years basking in the sunshine and watching some of the most talented softball players in the nation.

When I am joined on the balcony (usually only briefly) by my hardworking friends and colleagues who kid me about "taking the day off in the sun," I retort that I am actually doing *research* at this very moment. After all, I am writing my dissertation on "sports and male identity." (A great thing about sociology is that everything is data.)

One spring day I was enjoying a beautifully played pitchers' duel between Cal's women and another top-ranked team. It was late in the game, with the score tied 1 to 1, when I was joined in my personal left-field pavilion by a friendly and gentle man who is nearing the end of a very successful career as a sociologist at the university. Suddenly, with a runner on first via a rare base-on-balls from the Cal pitcher, the batter drove the ball on a line into left-center field. The left fielder managed to run the ball down, turn, and fire a strike to the shortstop just at the edge of the infield, who in turn spun and threw perfectly, laser-like, to the plate, nailing the lead runner. What precision teamwork and execution! And the game was still tied!

My fellow fan smiled, as did I, and shook his head. "You know, it amazes me to see a woman throw like that. I always thought there was something about the female arm that made it impossible for a woman to throw like a man."

I'm eight years old, I'm playing Little League baseball for the first time, and my dad's the coach! My first tryout-practice is an exciting, confusing, scary affair, with what seems like hundreds of boys, all with identical green caps and leather mitts, facing each other in two long lines, throwing balls back and forth as fathers furiously race around coaching, criticizing, encouraging, demonstrating, and scrawling mysterious things on clipboards.

Later, at home, my father informs me that two boys on the team throw like girls, and that I, unfortunately, am one of them! By the next practice, he tells me, we will have corrected that problem. That evening, with glove and cap securely in place, I anxiously face my father on the front lawn. And we play catch, for quite a while. I am concentrating, working hard to throw correctly ("like a *man*"), pulling my arm back as far as I can and snapping the ball overhand, just past my ear. When I do this, it feels very strange—I really have very little control over the flight of the ball, and it hurts my shoulder a bit—but I am rewarded with the knowledge that *this is how men throw the ball*. If I learn this, I won't embarrass either myself or my father. When at times I inadvertently revert to what feels like a more natural and more easily controllable throwing style (more of a shot-put style, with hand and ball starting just behind the ear, and elbow leading the way), I am immediately rewarded with a return throw that sails far over my head and lands two or three houses down. "Run! *Run* after that ball! You won't have to chase it anymore when you quit throwing like a girl!"

Simple behavior modification, actually. And it worked—I learned very rapidly how to throw properly. But it wasn't really having to run after the ball that taught me; it was the threat to my very fragile sense of masculinity. The fear—oh, the *fear*—of being thought a sissy, a *girl*!

I was momentarily taken aback that a renowned sociologist would have a biological explanation for such a difference between women and men. I explained to him that, indeed, throwing "like a girl" is actually a more anatomically natural motion for the human arm. Throwing "like a man" is a learned action that, repeated over time, can actually seriously damage the arm.

A few years ago, a sportswriter informally surveyed major league pitchers to determine how many of those who had played in Little League as youngsters had been pitchers in their youth. The astounding answer was *zero*. Stories of Little Leaguers burning their arms out for life are common. The destruction of young shoulders and elbows has led some children's leagues to outlaw curve balls. Others have had adults take over all the pitching for eight- and nine-year-olds.

Throwing "like a man" is an unnatural act, an act that (like most "masculine" behavior) must be learned. I learned it at a very young age, as did most of my male peers. And while I was on the front lawn with Dad, my older sister Linda was God-knows-where, but certainly not playing ball. Only this past summer did she join a softball team and learn how to throw a ball. She's a natural athlete who had to wait until the age of thirty-one to get some simple coaching.

Things change far too slowly for some of us, but things *are* changing. People are changing. As we men begin to question the traditional meaning of masculinity and reject those aspects of the traditional male role that have been oppressive to others and destructive to ourselves,

As we men begin to question the traditional meaning of masculinity we discover new ways to be men.

we discover new ways to be men. After a fifteen-year break, I, for one, have taken up pitching a baseball to a friend who used to be a catcher. I throw exclusively submarine-style (almost underhand), which does not hurt my shoulder as overhand throwing always did. And we do it just for the simple joy of throwing and catching the ball.

As more and more women master skills (including playing sports) that are traditionally in male territory, our conceptions of masculinity and femininity are being challenged. While watching women play softball, my professor friend learned something about the social basis for traditional distinctions between men and women. My sister not only plays softball, but coaches her nine-year-old daughter's team, all of whose members she teaches to throw a ball accurately and safely. With this role model and a changing social context, her daughter, Jennifer, plays with an enjoyment and confidence that was never allowed her mother. She loves to play. And she even loves to be the "bat girl" for her father's city-league softball team. The first time she went to clear a bat away from home plate, she was confronted by a boy about her age who said to her derisively, "There's no such *thing* as a bat *girl*!"

"Watch me," she replied.

Part II

SEXUALITY AND POWER

In recent years, the public image of male athletes has been transformed from that of an idealized role model for youth to that of an irresponsible, selfish, and often violent sexual predator. Indeed, from Mike Tyson's rape conviction to the New England Patriots' locker-room harassment of reporter Lisa Olson; from the accusations of sexual assault against members of the Portland Trailblazers pro basketball team to the youthful Spur Posse's tallying of their sexual "conquests" of young women, we have been inundated with stories of individual sexual assaults, gang rapes, and heterosexual promiscuity among male athletes.

Until fairly recently, rapes by athletes were treated as deviant acts by a few sick individuals. But news reporters and the public are now beginning to ask if incidents like Tyson's rape or the Spur Posse's competitive promiscuity are not isolated at all, but rather manifestations of a larger pattern of sexual abuse of women by male athletes. Though no definitive national study has yet been conducted, a growing body of evidence strongly suggests that, at least among college students, male athletes are more likely than male nonathletes to rape acquaintances and to take part in gang rapes. Consider the following:

- Athletes participated in approximately one-third of 862 sexual assaults on United States campuses according to a 1988-1991 survey by the National Institute of Mental Health (Melnick, 1992).
- Of twenty-six gang rapes alleged to have occurred from 1980 to 1990, most involved fraternity brothers and varsity athletes, Chris O'Sullivan, a Bucknell University psychologist discovered (Guernsey, 1993).
- Among 530 college students, including 140 varsity athletes, the athletes had higher levels of sexual aggression toward women than the nonathletes, Mary Koss and John Gaines

(1993) found. Koss and Gaines concluded that campus rape-prevention programs should especially target athletic teams.

Compelling as this evidence is, we want to emphasize two points. First, *nothing inherent in men leads them to rape women*. Peggy Sanday, an anthropologist, and other researchers have found that there *are* rape-free societies in the world, and that they tend to be characterized by low levels of militarization, high levels of respect for women, high levels of participation by women in the economy and the political system, and high levels of male involvement in child care. Second, *nothing inherent in sports makes athletes especially likely to rape women. Rather, it is the way sports are organized to influence developing masculine identities and male peer groups that leads many male athletes to rape.*

The articles in this section illustrate several of the social and psychological processes at work in this masculinity-sports dynamic. A fundamental aspect of this dynamic is the fact that the culture of male athletes is often characterized by sexually aggressive verbal sparring among peers. Central to this group dynamic is the denigration of anything considered feminine. And integrally related to this misogyny is homophobia—"faggot" and "blow me" are put downs on a par with "woman." Through these ritual shows of dominance, boys create the boundaries around their in-group ("We are not women or faggots"), and they simultaneously create a hierarchy within the group: the most successful at the verbal sparring are the "men" in the group; the less successful are the feminized subordinates. Through this process, boys learn to talk about—and treat—females (and penetrated males) as dehumanized objects of male sexual aggression. Underlying this aggressive boasting among young males is often a ragged insecurity about their masculinity and their sexuality. Young males' individual insecurity, coupled with group sparring to show sexual dominance, too often translates into male athletes learning to treat women as objects of sexual conquest, and thus into rape and other forms of violence against women.

The culture of male athletes can change. And in some places it has begun to change. Rape prevention and sexual responsibility programs now involve athletes on a growing number of college campuses. For instance, Tom Jackson has worked with the athletic department at the University of Arkansas to develop a mandatory rape-education and prevention program for athletes. In the five years the program has been in place, he says, no athlete who has participated has been implicated in any sexual assault. Sandra Caron, at the University of Maine, has developed a highly successful program called Athletes for Sexual Responsibility and Rape Awareness. Through this program, male and female athletes together are initiating and facilitating dialogues among other students about rape, sexuality, and "safe sex." A similar program for student athletes has recently begun at Northeastern University. Programs like these suggest that male athletes can take an integral role in disentangling the confusing and destructive ways that our culture has intertwined sexual pleasure with power and violence, and in the process can help create a world in which sexuality is associated more strongly with pleasure, love, respect, and care.

REFERENCES

Melnick, Merrill, 1992. "Male Athletes and Sexual Assault," *Journal of Physical Education, Recreation and Dance*. (May-June) pp. 32-35.

Koss, Mary P. & John A. Gaines, 1993. "The Prediction of Sexual Aggression by Alcohol Use, Athletic Participation, and Fraternity Affiliation," *Journal of Interpersonal Violence* 8 (1) pp. 94-108.

Guernsey, Lisa, 1993. "More Campuses Offer Rape-Prevention Programs for Male Athletes," *Chronicle of Higher Education* (February 10) p. A37.

The Myth of the Sexual Athlete

DON SABO

The phrase "sexual athlete" commonly refers to male heterosexual virtuosity in the bedroom. Images of potency, agility, technical expertise, and an ability to attract and satisfy women come to mind. In contrast, the few former athletes who have seriously written on the subject, like Dave Meggyesy and Jim Bouton, and films such as *Raging Bull* and *North Dallas Forty*, depict the male athlete as sexually uptight, fixated on early adolescent sexual antics and exploitative of women. The former image of athletic virility, however, remains fixed within the popular imagination. Partly for this reason, little has been said about the *real* connections between sports and male sexuality.

LOCKER-ROOM SEX TALK

Organized sports were as much a part of my growing up as Cheerios, television, and homework. My sexuality unfolded within the all-male social world of sports where sex was always a major focus. I remember, for example, when as prepubertal boys I and my friends pretended to be shopping for baseball cards so we could sneak peeks at *Playboy* and *Swank* magazines at the newsstand. After practices, we would talk endlessly about "boobs" and what it must feel like to kiss and neck. Later, in junior high, we teased one another in the locker room about "jerking off" or being virgins, and there were endless interrogations about "how far" everybody was getting with their girlfriends.

Eventually, boyish anticipation spilled into *real* sexual relationships with girls, which, to my delight and confusion, turned out to be a lot more complex than I ever imagined. While sex (kissing, necking, and petting) got more exciting, it also got more difficult to figure out and talk about. Inside, all the boys, like myself, needed to love and be loved. We were awkwardly reaching out for intimacy. Yet we were telling one another to "catch feels," be cool, connect with girls but don't allow yourself to depend on them. When I was a high-school junior, the gang in the weight room once accused me of being wrapped around my girlfriend's finger. Nothing could be further from the truth, I assured them, and to prove it I broke up with her. I felt miserable about this at the time, and I still feel bad about it.

Within the college jock subculture, men's public protests against intimacy sometimes became exaggerated and ugly. I remember two teammates, drunk and rowdy, ripping girls' blouses off at a party and crawling on their bellies across the dance floor to look up skirts. Then there were the late Sunday morning breakfasts in the dorm. We jocks would usually all sit at one table listening to one braggart or another describe his sexual exploits of the night before. Though a lot of us were turned off by such boasting, ego-boosting tactics, we never openly criticized it. Stories of raunchy, or even abusive sex, real or fabricated, were also assumed to "win points." A junior fullback claimed to have defecated on a girl's chest after she passed out during intercourse. There were also some laughing reports of "gang-bangs".

When sexual relationships were "serious," that is, tempered by love and commitment, the unspoken rule was silence. Rarely did we young men share our feelings about women, our uncertainty about sexual performance, or our disdain for the crudeness and insensitivity of some of our teammates. I now see the tragic irony in this: we could talk about casual sex and about using, trivializing, or debasing women, but frank discussions about sexuality that unfolded within a loving relationship were taboo. Within the locker room subculture, sex and love were seldom allowed to mix. There was a terrible split between our inner needs and outer appearances, between our desire for love from women and our feigned indifference toward them.

SEX AS A SPORT

Organized sports provide a social setting in which gender (i.e., masculinity and femininity) learning melds with sexual learning. Our sense of "femaleness" or "maleness" influences the ways we see ourselves as sexual beings. Indeed, as we develop, sexual identity emerges as an extension of an already formed gender identity, and sexual behavior tends to conform to cultural norms. To be manly in sports, traditionally, means to be competitive, successful, dominating, aggressive, stoical, goal-directed, and physically strong. Many athletes accept this definition of masculinity and apply it in their relationships with women. Dating becomes a sport in itself, and "scoring," or having sex with little or no emotional involvement, is a mark of masculine achievement. Sexual relationships are games in which women are seen as opponents, and his scoring means her defeat. Too often, women are pawns in men's quests for status within the male pecking order. For many of us jocks, sexual relationships are about man as a hunter and woman as prey.

Why is this? What transforms us from boys who depend on women to men who misunderstand, alienate ourselves from, and sometimes mistreat women? One part of the problem is the expectation that we are supposed to act as though we want to be alone, like the cowboy who always rides off into the sunset alone. In sports, there is only one "most valuable player" on the team.

Too often this prevents male athletes from understanding women and their life experiences. Though women's voices may reach men's ears from the sidelines and grandstands, they remain distant and garbled by the clamor of male competition. In sports, communication gaps between the sexes are due in part to women's historical exclusion, from refusal to allow girls to play along with boys, and coaching practices which quarantine boys from the "feminizing" taint of female influence. One result of this isolation is that sexual myths flourish. Boys end up learning about girls and female sexuality from other males, and the information that gets transmitted within the male network is often inaccurate and downright sexist. As boys, we lacked a vocabulary of intimacy, which would have enabled us to better share sexual experiences with others. The locker-room language that filled our adolescent heads did not exactly foster insights into the true nature of women's sexuality—or our own, for that matter.

PERFORMANCE AND PATRIARCHY

Traditional gender learning and locker-room sexual myths can also shape men's lovemaking behavior. Taught to be "achievement machines," many athletes organize their energies and perceptions around a performance ethic that influences sexual relations. Men apply their goal-directedness and preoccupation with performance to their lovemaking. In the movie Joe, a sexually liberated woman tells her hard-hat lover that "making love isn't like running a fifty-yard dash."

Making intercourse the chief goal of sex limits men's ability to enjoy other aspects of sexual experience. It also creates problems for both men and their partners. Since coitus requires an erection, men pressure themselves to get and maintain erections. If erections do not occur, or men ejaculate too quickly, their self-esteem as lovers and men can be impaired. In fact, sex therapists tell us that men's preoccupation and anxieties about erectile potency and performance can cause the very sexual dysfunctions they fear.

It is important to emphasize that not only jocks swallow this limiting model of male sexuality. Sports are not the only social setting that promotes androcentrism and eroticism without emotional intimacy. Consider how male sexuality is developed in fraternities, motorcycle gangs, the armed forces, urban gangs, pornography, corporate advertising, MTV, magazines like *Playboy* or *Penthouse*, and the movies—to name but a few examples. These are not random and unrelated sources of traditional masculine values. They all originate in patriarchy.

Sexual relations between men and women in Western societies have been conducted under the panoply of patriarchal power. The sexual values that derive from patriarchy emphasize male dominance and the purely physical dimensions of the sex act while reducing women to delectable but expendable objects. An alternative conception of human sexuality, however, is also gaining ascendancy within the culture. Flowing out of women's experiences and based on egalitarian values, it seeks to integrate eroticism with love and commitment. It is deeply critical of the social forces that reduce women (and men) to sex objects, depersonalize relationships, and turn human sexuality into an advertising gimmick or commodity to be purchased. This is the sexual ethos proffered by the women's movement.

Today's young athletes don't seem as hooked as their predecessors on the hypermasculine image traditional sports have provided. Perhaps this is because alternative forms of masculinity and sexuality have begun to enter the locker-room subculture. More girls are playing sports than ever before, and coeducational athletic experiences are more common. As more women enter the traditionally male settings of sports, business, factories, and government, men are finding it more difficult to perceive women in only one dimension. Perhaps we are becoming better able to see them as fellow human beings and, in the process, we are beginning to search for alternative modes of being men.

WHAT DO MEN REALLY WANT (OR NEED)?

Most of us do not really know what it is we want from our sexual lives. Men seem torn between yearning for excitement and longing for love and intimacy. On one side, we feel titillated by the glitter of corporate advertising. Eroticism jolts our minds and bodies. We're sporadically attracted by the simple hedonism of the so-called sexual revolution and the sometimes slick, sometimes sleazy veil of pornography, soft and hard.

Many of us fantasize about pursuing eroticism without commitment; some actually live the fantasy. Yet more men are recently becoming aware of genuine needs for intimate relationships. We are beginning to recognize that being independent, always on the make and emotionally controlled, is not meeting our needs. Furthermore, traditional masculine behavior is certainly not meeting women's expectations or satisfying their emotional needs. More and more men are starting to wonder if sexuality can be a vehicle for expressing and experiencing love.

In our culture many men are suffering from sexual schizophrenia. Their minds lead them toward eroticism while their hearts pull them toward emotional intimacy. What they think they want rarely coincides with what they need. Perhaps the uneasiness and the ambivalence that permeate male sexuality are due to this root fact: the traditional certainties that men have used to define their manhood and sexuality no longer fit the realities of their lives. Until equality between the sexes becomes more of a social reality, no new model of a more humane sexuality will take hold.

As for me, I am still exploring and redefining my sexuality. Although I don't have all the answers yet, I do have direction. I am listening more closely to women's voices, turning my head away from the sexist legacy of the locker room and pursuing a profeminist vision of sexuality. I feel good to have stopped pretending that I enjoy being alone. I never did like feeling alone.

WOMEN IN THE MEN'S LOCKER ROOM?

MIKE MESSNER

On September 17, 1990, Lisa Olson, a reporter for the *Boston Herald*, entered the New England Patriots locker room for routine postgame interviews. Several players harassed her with lewd comments and sexually aggressive gestures.The following week, Sam Wyche, coach for the Cincinnati Bengals, barred a woman sportswriter from the team's locker room, in violation of the National Football League's long-standing equal-access rules.

In the days and weeks following these incidents, reporters and athletes debated the issue of women in men's locker rooms. One side argued that a female reporter's "right to access" to the locker room after games must be respected, so she could get her story and meet her deadline. The other side asserted that athletes should have a "right to privacy" in the locker room. The 48 percent of NFL players who opposed the presence of women in a men's locker room felt that the locker room should be a male preserve. Scott Campbell, quarterback for the Atlanta Falcons, said, "When women start playing in the NFL, then they should be allowed in the locker room." And Ron Wolfley, Phoenix Cardinals running back, put it this way: "The locker room is a sweaty place. You want to belch. Maybe you want to scratch. It doesn't seem like a good place for women to be" (King 1990).

But Danny Noonan, Dallas Cowboy defensive tackle, seemed to sum up the feelings of the sizable minority (39 percent) of players who favor letting female reporters in the locker room: "I don't know why all of a sudden now it's coming out. I thought that this stuff was resolved in the seventies" (King 1990). Indeed, in an informal survey I conducted among acquaintances and my students, the dominant reaction appeared to be a yawn and a slightly irritated sense of déjà vu: hadn't the female-reporters-in-the-locker-room issue been dealt with over a decade ago?

Why does this issue continue to surface every few years, often in the form of ugly confrontations between male players and women reporters? Is it simply a clash of rights—the female reporters' right to pursue their profession versus the players' right to privacy in the locker room? I think that the conflict is much deeper than this. In order to understand the persistence of this issue—and especially the depth of anger it seems to periodically bring out in male athletes—it is necessary to answer the following questions:

- What specific kinds of relationships do male athletes construct with each other?
- What do men talk about in locker rooms?
- What is the role of sexuality in male athletes' relationships with each other?
- How are men's relationships with each other shaped by—and, in turn, how do they shape—men's attitudes about women and their relationships with women?

LEARNING TO "DO WOMEN"

Contrary to the popular stereotype of the male athlete—a confident, heterosexually active man-among-men—most of the former athletes I interviewed recalled feeling extremely shy and "lame" around girls and young women. Several of these men reported that, during high school or college, they eventually developed ways to talk with girls despite their shyness. Eldon C. (all names here are pseudonyms) said that, in high school,

> I was lame, as they called it. So I didn't know how to do women so well. My stepmother threw a sixteenth birthday party for me and invited a lot of friends, and I remember that day, trying on a lot of the roles that I saw guys playing, and it kind of shocked me because the women took it seriously, you know. That was a big turning point for me. That meant it was possible [laughs]. . . .

Calvin H. described a similar transformation from tortured shyness with girls in high school to developing a "rap" with women in college:

> I was just scared, and bashful and shy. I did not know what to say or what to do. It was very uncomfortable . . . . Like, a girl likes you, but then, clamming up and not being able to communicate very effectively. This was a very bad time, 'cause you're always around a lot of girls at parties . . . . I was very uncomfortable in groups and with individuals. Finally I went off to college and went to the extreme of trying to attract a lot of girls, and was semi-successful. You knew you had to have a date on Fridays, and knew you had to have one on Saturdays, and so you just walked through the student union, and you'd just have this rap you'd thought of, and you'd just put it on. It was peer pressure . . . . I'm naturally a shy person, but somehow in

"There's no excuse for what happened in the locker room."

Victor Kiam

I am appalled by what reportedly happened on September 17th to Lisa Olson in the New England Patriots' locker room. Male chauvinism, gross behavior of any sort...I detest. Rape-physical, mental, threatened, hinted at or joked about—is something I will not stand for.

The NFL is conducting a full investigation of this incident and I support that 100%. Please remember, the New England Patriot's team and organization are comprised of many outstanding individuals.

> college I was able to somehow fall into the right kinds of things to do and say . . . .

We can see from these stories that developing a "rap" with women becomes an almost ritualized way that a young man can help himself overcome an otherwise paralyzing shyness, a sense of "lameness" when trying to relate to young women. This verbal game involves a conscious self-manipulation ("You'd just put it on"), and one result is that girls and women become the objects of men's verbal manipulation.

This verbal manipulation of women does not spring naturally or magically from men's shyness; it is socially learned. Notice that Eldon C. learned to "do women" by watching his male peers. And Calvin H., though somewhat mystified as to how he was able to overcome his shyness and "fall into the right things to say," also cites "peer pressure" as a motivating force. Clearly, an analysis of how men's sexual relationships with women develop must take into account attitudes and feelings in male peer groups about sexuality and emotional commitment to women.

THE "SPERMATIC ECONOMY"

Peter Lyman, in his study of male college fraternities, argues that the fraternal bond in all-male social groups has an erotic basis (Lyman 1987). In the past, the key to maintaining the male bond was the denial of the erotic. Organized sports, as they arose in the late nineteenth and early twentieth centuries, were based in part on a Victorian antisexual ethic. This ethic comprised two beliefs. First, all-male social institutions such as sports were thought to "masculinize" young males in an otherwise "feminized" culture, thus preventing homosexuality.

A second popular (and "scientific") belief concerned the "spermatic economy." Victorians held that "the human male possessed a limited quantity of sperm which could be invested in various enterprises, ranging from business through sport to copulation and procreation. In this context, the careful regulation of the body was the only path to the conservation of energy" (Mrozek 1983, 20). In other words, young men's precious energies would be drained off should they expend too much sperm. As Todd Crosset (1990) has pointed out, sports were considered the key "to regenerate the male body and thus make efficient use of male energy."

Some of the older men in my study went through adolescence and early adulthood when the remnants of the ideology of the "spermatic economy" were still alive. Eldon C. said that, as a young runner from the late 1940s through the mid-1950s, he had been "a bit cautious about sex, because I still had some old-fashioned notions about sexual energy [being] competitive with athletic stuff."

Most of the men I interviewed, though, came of age during the sexual revolution of the 1960s and early 1970s, when the dominant credo became "If it feels good, do it." As a result, the athletic male peer group became a setting in which sexual activity and talk of sexual activity (real or imagined) was a key component of the peer status system.

If the bond among men is erotic, and the culture is increasingly telling them that "if it feels good, do it," what is to prevent the development of sexual relations among these young men who are playing, showering, dressing and living in such close quarters together? The answer is overt homophobia and the enforced displacement of the erotic towards women as objects of sexual talk and practice. In boyhood, adolescent, and young adult male peer groups, "fag," "girl," and "woman" are insults that are used almost interchangeably. Through this practice, heterosexual masculinity is collectively constructed by denigrating homosexuality and femininity as "not-male." Bill S. described how his male peers in high school helped him to structure his own public presentation of his sexuality:

> I was shy [with girls]. But you *gotta* be involved to the point where you get 'em into bed, you know, you *fuck 'em*, or something like that, yeah, that's real important [laughs]. Just so I could prove my heterosexuality it was real important. I wanted to be able to have the *body*, and the sort of friends around who admired me in some sort of way, to have that pull.

Using women as objects of sexual conquest is important for gaining status in the male peer group, but also tends to impoverish young males' relationships with females. As Bob G. put it, he and his high-school friends would "tell a lot of stories about girls. I guess it was a way to show our masculinity. But I never got emotionally involved with any of the girls I went out with. I never got close to any of them." The link between young males' tendency to "tell [sexual] stories about girls" and their lack of intimacy with girls is an important one. As Peter Lyman (1987, 151) points out, young males commonly use sexually aggressive stories and hostile jokes as a means of "negotiating" the "latent tension and aggression they feel toward each other."

Relationships with male teammates may not only influence a young man's attitudes toward women, but may also distort his relationships with women and subordinate these relationships to that with the team. Some athletes end up like former pro-football star Jim Brown: when Brown played football for the Cleveland Browns, he explained in his book, *Out of Bounds* (1989, 190), his male teammates started calling him "the Hawk" because he was so successful in "chasing women." At age fifty-three, Brown continued to view and to treat women primarily as young, sexual bodies to be consumed: "My lady right now is nineteen . . . . When I eat a peach, I don't want it overripe. I want that peach when it's peaking" (Brown 1989, 183-84). This attitude keeps men like Brown from developing a long-term intimate relationship with one woman. After all, every woman ages; her body changes. But she can be discarded and replaced by what Brown and other men see as an endless supply of younger, firmer bodies.

SEXUAL SCHIZOPHRENIA

Many male athletes yearn for, and manage to develop, a more or less exclusive relationship with one woman. But this happens despite the fact that the male peer group tends to police its own members concerning their intimacy with females. Male peers might tell a boy or young man who is spending too much time with a girlfriend—who is becoming too attached—that he is "pussywhipped," as Don Sabo has discussed in "The Myth of the Sexual Athlete."

In a study of two college male locker rooms, Timothy Curry (1991) found that sexually aggressive talk about women usually takes the form of loud public performance. Curry also observed that any private discussions between two men about actual relationships with girlfriends usually take place in hushed tones, and often at the edges of the locker room. If this sort of talk is discovered by the group, the speakers are often ridiculed and taunted to reveal details about the woman's body and tell whether or not she is sexually "putting out."

The result of this locker-room subculture is, for some young men, sexual schizophrenia: they keep their emotional attachment with females a secret while participating in aggressive sexual talk with their male peers in the locker room.

The need to prove one's manhood through sexual conquests of women is experienced as a burden by many young heterosexual men, but it is especially oppressive for gay athletes. The pressure to be seen by one's peers as "a man"—indeed, the pressure to see one's self as "a man"—makes most young males play along with the homophobic and sexist locker-room banter. But gay men are far more likely than heterosexual men to perceive this behavior as a strategy for constructing an

The bonds that develop among male athletes are often premised on the devaluation of women and of homosexual men.

identity. As Brittan (1989, 41) explains, "Most heterosexuals do not have to do too much identity work because they tend to function in contexts in which heterosexuality is taken for granted."

In the locker room, gay athletes must constantly engage in "identity work." Nearly every gay athlete interviewed by Brian Pronger (1990, 195) agreed that being around all of those naked male bodies in the locker room "feed[s] the homoerotic imagination and provide[s] homoerotic contact." One gay athlete told Pronger (1990, 199) that there is "a surprising amount of sexual cruising and activity in the university locker rooms and shower. I've certainly had sex there." But since homosexual behavior—or even covert expressions of desire—violate locker-room norms, most gay men develop an ironic strategy of identity construction: while superficially conforming to the heterosexist masculine culture, they view this culture through their hidden knowledge of the highly charged eroticism of the locker room.

RAPE CULTURE

A few of the heterosexual men whom I interviewed objected to—and eventually rejected—the sexism and homophobia of the jock subculture. But they were rare exceptions to the rule. For young men who truly wanted athletic careers, rejecting one of the key bonds to the male peer group would have ruined their chances of success. So whether they liked the sexism and homophobia or not, most went along with these things. And when verbal sparring and bragging about sexual conquests led to actual behavior, peer group values encouraged these young men to treat females as objects of conquest. This sort of masculine peer group dynamic is at the heart of what feminists have called "the rape culture" (Herman 1984; Beneke 1982). Eugene Kanin's (1984) study of date rape revealed that college men who have experienced pressure from their current male friends to engage in sexual activity are more likely to rape female acquaintances. Similarly, in a national study Mary Koss and Thomas Dinero (1990) found that "involvement in peer groups that reinforce highly sexualized views of women," such as varsity athletics and fraternities, is an important predictor of "sexually aggressive behavior" by college males. And Robin Warshaw (1988, 112) concluded from her research on acquaintance rape that "athletic teams are breeding grounds for rape [because they] are often populated by men who are steeped in sexist, rape-supportive beliefs." Between 1983 and 1986, in fact, a U.S. college athlete was reported for sexual assault on an average of once every eighteen days (Warshaw 1988, 113).

The sexual objectification of women on which male athletes base their friendships with one another is probably, in most cases, just a rhetorical performance; it does not necessarily reflect or cause actual physical aggression against women. But the fact that the locker room is the main site in which male athletes use sexism and homophobia to "safely" forge erotic bonds among themselves helps to explain the vehemence with which men often defend this "turf" against female reporters. The fragile basis of men's bonding through erotic shows of dominance in the locker room can be disrupted by the presence of competent, professional women (rather than debased, sexualized objects). Unless and until the kind of masculinity that is developed in the locker room is radically transformed, female sports reporters, I fear, will continue to face covert barriers and, at times, overt sexual harassment in the locker room.

REFERENCES

Beneke, T. 1982. *Men on Rape*. New York: St. Martin's.

Brittan, A. 1989. *Masculinity and Power*. New York: Blackwell.

Brown, J. 1989. *Out of Bounds*. New York: Kensington.

Crosset, T. 1990. "Masculinity, Sexuality, and the Development of Early Modern Sport," pp. 45-54. In *Sport, Men and the Gender Order: Critical Feminist Perspectives*, ed. M. A. Messner & D. F. Sabo. Champaign, IL: Human Kinetics.

Curry, T. J. 1991. "Fraternal Bonding in the Locker Room: A Feminist Analysis of Talk about Competition and Women." *Sociology of Sport Journal* 8:119-35.

Herman, D. 1984. "The Rape Culture." In *Women: A Feminist Perspective*, 3rd ed., ed. J. Freeman. Palo Alto, CA: Mayfield.

Kanin, E. J. 1984. "Date Rape: Differential Sexual Socialization and Relative Deprivation." *Victimology* 9: 95-108.

King, P. 1990. "Curtain Call." *Sports Illustrated*, October 15:38-40, 43.

Koss, M. P., and T. E. Dinero. 1988. "Predictors of Sexual Aggression among a National Sample of Male College Students." In *Human Sexual Aggression: Current Perspectives, Annals of the New York Academy of Sciences*, ed. R. A. Prentky and V. Quinsey. 528:133-46.

Lyman, P. 1987. "The Fraternal Bond as a Joking Relationship: A Case Study of Sexist Jokes in Male Group Bonding." In *Changing Men: New Directions in Research on Men and Masculinity*, ed. M. S. Kimmel, 148-63. Newbury Park, CA: Sage.

Mrozek, D. J. 1983. *Sport and the American Mentality: 1880-1910*. Knoxville, University of Tennessee.

Pronger, B. 1990. *The Arena of Masculinity: Sports, Homosexuality, and the Meaning of Sex*. New York: St. Martin's.

Sabo, D. 1989. "The Myth of the Sexual Athlete." In *Changing Men: Issues in Gender, Sex, and Politics*, 20.

Warshaw, R. 1988. *I Never Called It Rape*. New York: Harper and Row.

Sin & Redemption: The Sugar Ray Leonard Wife-Abuse Story

MIKE MESSNER AND WILLIAM SOLOMON

On March 30, 1991, the *Los Angeles Times* broke a story, based on divorce court documents, that Sugar Ray Leonard had admitted to physically abusing his wife, including hitting her with his fists, and to using cocaine and alcohol over a three-year period while temporarily retired from boxing. Despite the fact that stories of sexual violence, drug abuse, and other criminal activities by famous athletes had become commonplace items in the sports pages, these particular revelations shocked many people, because Leonard had been an outspoken advocate for "just say no to drugs" campaigns and he publicly had traded on his image as a good family man (e.g., by posing with his son in a soft drink TV commercial). Thus, revelations of his violence and drug abuse left him open to charges of hypocrisy, to public humiliation, and to permanent loss of his status as a hero.

FRAMING THE STORY

We decided to explore how this story was "framed" by three major newspapers. By a "news frame," we mean the way the media assign meaning to an event or occurrence, by deciding whether or not to report something, and what details to highlight, ignore, or deemphasize. A news frame is therefore an inherently ideological construct, but it rarely appears so. This is because, although news frames ultimately impose preferred meanings on a story, these meanings are commonly drawn from socially shared (hegemonic) understandings of the world (Solomon, 1992).

We analyzed coverage of the Sugar Ray Leonard story in two national dailies, the *Los Angeles Times* (LAT) and the *New York Times* (NYT), as well as in the now defunct specialized paper the *National Sports Daily* (NSD). We collected all news stories and editorial columns in the three papers until the story "died out" as a major news item. This took nine days, from March 30, 1991, until April 7, 1991. Next, we analyzed the contents of the stories. Our overriding concern was to examine how the story was framed as a "drug story," a "domestic violence" story, or both.

Our analysis of the three newspapers revealed three stages in the development of the news frame. Stage One was day one, when LAT broke the story. Stage Two was days two and three, when all three papers covered Sugar Ray Leonard's press conference and "reactions" inside and outside of the boxing world. Stage Three was days three through nine, when follow-up stories and editorial commentary discussed the "meanings" of the story.

STAGE 1: THE BREAKING STORY

The LAT broke the story and featured it as the top sports story of the day. The headline read, "Leonard Used Cocaine, His Former Wife Testifies," while the subhead stated that "Sugar Ray confirms he abused her physically, acknowledges drug and alcohol abuse." The accompanying photo, of the couple smiling and about to kiss each other, was captioned, "Juanita and Sugar Ray Leonard, pictured before their divorce, testified about marital violence and substance abuse."

Although the wife-abuse issue clearly was a central part of the story, the headlines and the paragraphs that followed revealed a subtle asymmetry in the coverage of the "drug angle" and the "violence angle." The opening paragraph stated that although Leonard "appeared in nationally televised antidrug public service announcements in 1989 [he] has used cocaine himself . . . ." When Leonard's violence toward his wife was introduced in the third paragraph of the story, we read that Leonard confirmed that "he abused her physically *because of* alcohol and drug abuse" (italics ours). This was a key moment in the initial framing of the story: Leonard admitted to abusing drugs and alcohol, which in turn caused him to abuse his wife.

Now that the story was tentatively framed as one about "drug abuse," several paragraphs of sometimes graphic testimony from Maryland divorce-court records followed. In her testimony, Juanita Leonard said that over a two-year period Sugar Ray Leonard often struck her with his fists, and that he would "throw me around" and "harass me physically and mentally in front of the children." He threatened to shoot himself; he threw lamps and broke mirrors. He once scared her so much that she attempted to leave the house with the children: "I was holding my six-month-old child and [Leonard] spit in my face. He pushed me. He shoved me . . . . I was on my way out the door. He wouldn't let me out. He took a can of kerosene and poured it on the front foyer floor in our house. He told me he was going to burn the house down . . . that he wasn't going to let me leave the house or anything." Sugar Ray Leonard, in his testimony, did not deny any of this. He agreed that he sometimes threatened her and struck her with his fists. Despite the newspaper's initial effort to employ a "drug story" frame, the graphic, emotionally gripping testimony about domestic violence left open the possibility that the story could have developed into one about wife abuse. As the story broke, then, the "drug story" frame was still very much in the making, and potentially open to contest.

STAGE 2: PUBLIC ISSUES & PRIVATE MATTERS

On days two and three, the "drug story" news frame was solidified, and the "wife-abuse story" was rapidly marginalized. On day two, the LAT and NYT ran major articles covering the press conference that Sugar Ray Leonard held to discuss the revelations about his drug abuse and family violence. On day three, the NSD ran a story covering the news conference. The headlines of these stories stated, "Leonard Says He Used Cocaine After Injury" (LAT), "Leonard Tells of Drug Use" (NYT), and "Sugar Ray Tells Bitter Tale of Cocaine Abuse" (NSD). None of the headlines, subheads, or lead paragraphs mentioned wife abuse. The photos that ran with the articles showed a somber Leonard apparently wiping a tear from his cheek as he spoke at the press conference. None of the photo captions mentioned wife abuse.

The first seven paragraphs of the LAT story detailed Leonard's explanations of how and why he began to abuse drugs and alcohol after his eye injury and retirement, and chronicled his statements that his drug use was "wrong . . . childish . . . stupid." The story also highlighted the fact that "as a role model, he advised that cocaine use is 'not the right road to take,' adding, 'It doesn't work. I'll be the first to admit it. I hope they look at my mistake—and don't use it.' " Finally, in the eighth paragraph, the writer noted that Leonard "declined" to discuss "the physical abuse or suicide threats alleged by his former wife, Juanita, last summer during questioning under oath" before the couple reached a multimillion-dollar divorce settlement. The story did not mention Leonard's corroboration, under oath, of his wife's "allegations" of abuse. Instead, it quoted Leonard's statement at the press conference that he would "be lying" if he were to say that he and his wife never "fought, argued, or grabbed each other," but "that was in our house, between us. Unfortunately, during the proceedings, which are very emotional and very painful, certain things are taken out of context or exaggerated." At this point, the violence issue was dropped from the story for good. For the next eight paragraphs, the story returned to explanations of Leonard's drug abuse. The final six paragraphs chronicled his statements of remorse for his drug abuse ("I stand here ashamed, hurt"), and his statements that his drug abuse is now a thing of the past ("I grew up"). The NYT essentially followed suit in framing this news as a "drug story" and almost entirely ignoring Leonard's abuse of his wife.

The NSD story on the press conference went even farther than the LAT and NYT in framing the story almost exclusively as a "drug story." The first eight paragraphs discussed Leonard's admission of drug and alcohol abuse, and noted that once he came out of his retirement and boxed again, his drug abuse ended. "I was again doing what I loved best—fighting," Leonard stated in the story. "I became a better father and person without the use of a substitute." The only mention of wife abuse was in the ninth paragraph: "He also physically abused his wife, Juanita, according to sealed divorce documents." Immediately following this sentence was an abrupt change of subject as the story continued, "Leonard said he did not go to a treatment center to stop." This jarring switch testifies to the extent to which this story had become almost entirely a "drug story." The writer did not see a need to explain, after mentioning wife abuse, that he was referring to a treatment center not for stopping wife abuse, but rather for stopping drug use. Wife abuse was outside the frame.

STAGE 3: REDEMPTION

During the next week, all three papers ran follow-ups and editorial commentaries on the Sugar Ray Leonard story. The dominant theme of nearly all of these stories was that Leonard's redemption from his drug abuse was another stage in a heroic career. On April 1, the NSD ran an opinion column headlined, "This is the Truth about Sugar Ray: He's Not Perfect, but then Who is?" The column celebrated the "love affair" that the people of the United States had had with Leonard: "In Montreal, he fought for us . . . . We applauded [his] courage and we were intoxicated with inspiration . . . . We loved Leonard. We truly did." The column went on to describe the "shock" that "we" all felt at the revelations of Leonard's cocaine use. But the focus of the column was on Leonard's redemption and our "compassion" for him. When we make heroes of athletes, the writer argued, we set them up to "fall down." Nowhere in the column was there mention of wife abuse.

The next day, the LAT ran an opinion column, by the reporter who originally broke the story, headlined "Act of Courage Didn't Involve a Single Punch." In the column, the writer admiringly recalled Leonard's many "acts of courage" in the ring, and argued that Leonard showed this courage again at his press conference, "under the most difficult of circumstances, when he admitted he had used cocaine." In an almost breathless tone, the writer continually mentioned Leonard's "courage" (nine times), his "bravery" (three times) and his "intelligence." He never mentioned wife abuse. Leonard was more than redeemed in the eyes of this writer. In fact, this "difficult" incident appears to have further elevated Leonard's status, from the reporter's point of view: "The man and his courage. It was a class act." The same day, the NYT ran a similar story, headlined "Leonard Hears Words of Support," which mentioned wife abuse only in passing. The first paragraph expressed the focus of the article: "The reaction of the boxing world to Sugar Ray Leonard's acknowledgment that he used cocaine and drank heavily in the early 1980s had been mostly sympathetic." The dominant news frame clearly had solidified: in all three newspapers, "wife abuse" was either completely ignored or marginalized as outside the "drug story" frame.

WITHIN THE FRAME: SIN AND REDEMPTION

By the end of the 1980s, stories about athletes on drugs had become so commonplace that they were seldom thought of as big news. In addition, the sports media had constructed an ideological news frame for jocks-on-drugs stories that turned these stories into moral dramas of individual sin and redemption. The jock-on-drugs drama came to follow a formula:

1) revelations of sin and subsequent public humiliation;
2) shameful confession and promises to never take drugs again;
3) public evangelism to children to "say no" to drugs; and
4) public redemption.

This formula reflects the ideology underlying the Reagan administration's "just say no" to drugs campaigns of the 1980s. These campaigns were largely successful in framing drug problems (and their solutions) as issues of individual moral choice, rather than as social

The sports media quickly accepted Leonard's tearful apology for having abused drugs and alcohol, and chose to ignore or quickly explain away his violent abuse of his former wife.

problems resulting from growing poverty, the deterioration of cities and schools, or general alienation and malaise. Sports reporters appear to have uncritically accepted this framework of meaning and adapted it to the otherwise thorny social issue of jocks on drugs. Moreover, athletes quickly learned to act out their prescribed parts in this morality play, as Sugar Ray Leonard's tearful press conference aptly demonstrated.

When the drama is properly played out, within a year or so following the initial public revelation of drug use, the athlete is often reinstated as a sports player (some athletes—such as Steve Howe, a baseball player—have managed to cycle through this drama several times). Leonard was fortunate in that the public revelation of his drug and alcohol abuse occurred several years after his "sins" took place. That he could tearfully (and, we are left to assume, honestly) admit that he committed these sins *in the past* meant that there could be a blurring simultaneity to the movement through the drama's stages. The day after the public revelations, Leonard himself shamefully confessed, apologized, swore that he had not taken drugs for a long time, and evangelized to youths to "say no" to drugs. Within a few days, playing out their own part in the drama, the sports media granted Leonard full redemption from his sins.

OUTSIDE THE FRAME

By the third day of the Sugar Ray Leonard story, wife abuse was so entirely outside the dominant "drug story" frame that several follow-up stories and editorials did not mention it at all. But the details about wife abuse were not entirely forgotten. They continued to appear, albeit always very briefly, in some follow-up stories and commentary. Mention of wife abuse, when it appeared, was couched in language similar to the following sentence from a follow-up NYT story: ". . . his former wife, Juanita, [said] that Leonard used cocaine on occasion and physically mistreated her while under the influence of alcohol." This sentence demonstrates the three ways that the facts of wife abuse were handled when they appeared within the "drug story" news frame:

1) *The violence was presented in neutralizing language:* The graphic descriptions of Sugar Ray Leonard's violence—

his threats involving guns and kerosene, his spitting in his wife's face, his hitting her with his fists, and so on—that appeared in the original divorce testimony were replaced with more vague and neutral language: Leonard "physically mistreated" his wife.

2) *Sugar Ray Leonard's admitted acts of violence were presented not as facts but as Juanita Leonard's "claims:"* although Leonard clearly had acknowledged in the divorce testimony that he had committed the acts of violence of which his wife accused him, in nearly all of the follow-up stories these acts were presented as incidents that Juanita Leonard "said," "claimed," or "alleged" had occurred. The writers did not add that Sugar Ray Leonard had acknowledged having committed these acts, thus leaving the impression, perhaps, that these were merely Juanita Leonard's "claims," or "allegations," not "facts."

3) *A causal relationship between drug and alcohol abuse and wife abuse was incorrectly implied:* nearly every mention of the wife abuse incidents in the follow-up commentaries implied that drug and alcohol abuse caused Leonard to act violently against his wife. Most often, the articles did not directly argue this causal relationship ("Drugs made him hit her"); rather, they implied the relationship by always linking any mention of his "mistreatment" of his wife with the observation that he had been abusing drugs. Astonishingly, reporters appear to have relied entirely on the testimony of Sugar Ray and Juanita Leonard to conclude, all too easily and quickly, that the drug and alcohol abuse caused the wife abuse to happen.

The writers apparently never consulted experts on domestic violence, who undoubtedly would have made two important points. First, reports by wife abusers, and by abused wives, on why wife abuse has occurred, are generally suspect (Dobash *et al.* 1992). Wayne Ewing (1982), who works with and studies men who batter women, argues that these couples' relationships are usually characterized by a common "cycle of violence" that includes "the building of tension and conflict; the episode of battering; the time of remorse; the idyllic time of reconciliation." In the stage of remorse, the male batterer typically denies responsibility for the act of battery. As Ewing puts it, "There is no shock of recognition in the cycle of violence. It is not a matter of 'Oh my God, did I do that?' It is a matter of *stating* 'Oh my God, I couldn't have done that,' implying that I in fact did not do it . . . . Remorse, in this model of 'making things right' again literally wipes the slate clean." For the victim who decides, for whatever reason, to remain in a relationship with her batterer, the stage of reconciliation in the cycle of violence often involves at least a partial acceptance of this denial of responsibility: "The man who hit me is not the *real* man I love, and who loves me." Within this context of denial, alcohol or other drugs can become convenient scapegoats: "It was the booze talking" (and hitting), not the man.

Second, research on domestic violence has found no evidence that alcohol abuse causes wife abuse. Numerous studies have shown a statistical correlation between heavy drinking (especially alcoholic binging) and wife abuse. But the "drunken bum" theory of wife abuse is largely a myth: only about one out of four instances of wife abuse involves alcohol (Kantor and Strauss, 1987). In fact, in cases where binge drinking and wife abuse occur together, both may result from what researchers have called a frustrated "power motivation" in husbands (McClelland *et al.* 1972). Indeed, research suggests that men who are most likely to commit acts of wife abuse are those most firmly enmeshed in "the cultural tradition which glorifies violence, assumes male dominance, and tolerates violence by men against women" (Kantor and Strauss 1987, 225). This sounds remarkably like a description of the world of men's sports, in general, and of boxing in particular (Gorn 1986; Messner 1992; Sabo 1985).

Similarly, Ewing points to a general culture of male dominance and a "civic advocacy of violence" as the main antecedents of men's violence against women. He argues that "[w]ith respect to the psychological makeup of the abusive male, there is considerable consensus that these men evidence low self-esteem, dependency needs, unfamiliarity with their emotions, fear of intimacy, poor communication skills and performance orientation." This description of the male batterer sounds quite similar to the psychological profile of recently retired male athletes (Messner 1992).

The sports media apparently never entertained the idea that masculine emotional socialization, including a toleration of violence, along with a loss of self-esteem brought on by an insecure public status might be at the root of both Leonard's misuse of drugs and alcohol and his abuse of his wife. To consider this possibility, of course, would have entailed questioning the system of patriarchal values that underlies institutionalized sports. Moreover, this line of analysis inevitably would invite serious questioning of the role of violence in sports, and the possible links between violence in sports with violence in personal life. Young U.S. males grow up in a society that accepts, even celebrates, violence. Sports such as boxing, football, and hockey are surely conveying a pro-violence message to young males (Messner 1992; Sabo and Panepinto 1990). And, given the misogyny that is built into the dominant subculture of men's sports, the advocacy and celebration of men's athletic violence against each other too often becomes directly translated into violence against women—violence that is often sexualized (Koss and Dinero 1988; Sabo 1986; Warshaw 1988).

In the case of Sugar Ray Leonard, sportswriters might have examined the possible links between two facts: first, here is a man who won fame and fortune by successfully battering other men with his fists; second, once out of the sports limelight, because of what appeared to be a career-ending injury, he turned to battering his own body with drugs and alcohol, and the body of his wife with his fists. This line of reasoning would draw together what Michael Kaufman (1987) has called "the triad of men's violence": violence against other men, violence against one's self, and violence against women.

That these links were never acknowledged illustrates the extent to which newspapers still form a symbiotic economic alliance with organized sports. But it would be wrong to suspect a conscious conspiracy to cover up Leonard's abuse of his wife. The adoption of the "drug story" frame and the marginalization of the "wife abuse" frame are logical results of sports reporters' immersion—probably largely unconscious—in a hegemonic ideology based in corporate and patriarchal relations of power. Denial of men's violence against women, especially that which occurs in families, is still widespread in our society (Kurz 1989). Newspaper sports departments, especially, are still relatively unaffected by feminism. Overwhelmingly male, they have been much slower to admit women than non-sports news departments. The Association for Women in Sports Media estimates that 9,650 of the approximately 10,000 U.S. print and broadcast journalists are men (Nelson 1991).

We wonder how the Sugar Ray Leonard story might have been differently framed if women made up a large proportion of newspaper sports departments. There is some evidence that female sports reporters approach their stories from a more "human," less "technical" point of view than male sports reporters (Mills 1988: 229). But we suspect that simply changing the sex composition of the sports newsroom would not drastically change the relative values placed on men's and women's sports. Indeed, it is difficult to imagine a less sexist sports newsroom in the absence of a feminist revolution throughout the sports world.

REFERENCES

Dobash, R. P., R. E. Dobash, M. Wilson, and M. Daly. 1992. "The Myth of Sexual Symmetry in Marital Violence." *Social Problems* 39: 79-91.

Ewing, W. 1982. "The Civic Advocacy of Violence." *M: Gentle Men for Gender Justice* 8: 5-7, 22.

Gorn, E. J. 1986. *The Manly Art: Bare-Knuckle Prize Fighting in America*. Ithaca: Cornell University Press.

Kantor, G. K. and M. A. Straus. 1987. "The 'Drunken Bum' Theory of Wife Beating." *Social Problems* 34: 213-230.

Kaufman, M. 1987. "The Construction of Masculinity and the Triad of Men's Violence." In *Beyond Patriarchy: Essays by Men on Pleasure, Power, and Change*, ed. M. Kaufman, 1-29. Toronto: Oxford University Press.

Koss, M. P. and T. E. Dinero. 1988. "Predictors of Sexual Aggression among a National Sample of Male College Students." In *Human Sexual Aggression: Current Perspectives, Annals of the New York Academy of Sciences*, ed. R. A. Prentsky and V. Quinsey. 528: 133-146.

Kurz, D. 1989. "Social Science Perspectives on Wife Abuse: Current Debates and Future Directions." *Gender & Society* 3: 489-505.

McClelland, D. C., W. N. Davis, R. Kalin, and E. Warner. 1972. *The Drinking Man*. New York: The Free Press.

Messner, M. A. 1992. *Power at Play: Sports and the Problem of Masculinity*. Boston: Beacon Press.

Mills, K. 1988. *A Place in the News: From Women's Pages to the Front Page*. New York: Columbia University Press.

Nelson, M. B. 1991. *Are We Winning Yet?: How Women Are Changing Sports and Sports Are Changing Women*. New York: Random House.

Sabo, D. 1986. "Pigskin, Patriarchy and Pain." *Changing Men: Issues in Gender, Sex and Politics* 16: 24-25.

Sabo, D. and J. Panepinto. 1990. "Football Ritual and the Social Production of Masculinity." In *Sport, Men and the Gender Order: Critical Feminist Perspectives*, ed. M. A. Messner and D. F. Sabo, 115-26. Champaign, IL: Human Kinetics.

Solomon, W. S. 1992. "News Frames and Media Packages: Covering El Salvador." *Critical Studies in Mass Communication* 9:56-74.

Warshaw, R. 1988. *I Never Called It Rape*. New York: Harper and Row.

Riding with the Spur Posse

MIKE MESSNER

Recently, quite a media stir occurred when several girls and young women publicly accused members of the self-named Spur Posse, at Lakewood High School in Long Beach, California, of rape. The boys in the Posse bond with each other by competitively tabulating their sexual conquests of women as "points" scored against one another. To the Posse members, this is all in fun: "If somebody has 60 points," one Posse member explained, "somebody else wants to catch up. But it ain't rape. You'd even count your girlfriend as a point. We'd come back from Vegas and say, 'I'm 44 now. I'm Reggie Jackson.' That's how we did it."

Hearing the story of the Spur Posse and seeing its unapologetic, even boastful members on TV talk shows led me to muse about some of my own experiences as a young athlete. I see striking similarities between my peer group back then and the Posse today: most obviously, sports metaphors continue to permeate the language of sexual conquest, just as they did when I was a young jock. One jarring difference, though, is that in my day the guys competed with each other to "get to second base" or, at most, to "third base." Today, apparently only "home runs" count.

The following story is a somewhat fictionalized re-creation of my own experiences over twenty years ago. In the story, I purposely use the same misogynous language and ways of talking about women and sex that characterized my athletic male peer group at that time.

Reexamined in the light of over two decades of feminist thought and activism, my story illustrates several things about the social construction of a certain kind of male heterosexuality. First of all, as Jack Litewka pointed out in his insightful 1977 essay "The Socialized Penis," boys and young men learn from each other, and often from pornography, a dominant "sexual script." Through this script, young males essentially train their own minds and bodies to become sexually aroused through a three-stage process: objectification of a woman, fixation on one or more of her erotically charged body parts, and conquest through real or imagined sexual intercourse. In this process, the girl or woman, in the male's mind, is reduced to a manipulated object and fragmented into a set of body parts that the male uses to excite himself. Importantly, the sexual act is most erotically salient for the young man in terms of his status vis-a-vis his male peers—not in relation to his actual sexual partner. Though she is physically present, the girl or woman, as a thinking, choosing partner, is obliterated. She serves as the conquered object through which the guys have "sex" with each other. Clearly, this approach to sexual relations with women lies at the heart of acquaintance rape and gang rape.

THROWN OUT STEALING SECOND

Tonight, I was finally gonna get some action. I had a hot date with this new girl, Sue, and I'd had been telling myself and my buddy Will all week that this time I was gonna score like never before. In fact, "Never Before" was getting to be a pretty sore spot with me. Here I was in the middle of my freshman year of college, and still a virgin. This basketball season just past, I had taken all kinds of shit from teammates for being one of the two "team virgins." During that time, Will and I had bet several six-packs of beer over who would score the most and soonest with his respective girlfriend, but we both remained stuck at "first base" (kissing) for months. Our bets were based on who would first reach "second base" (touching bare tits—just touching the outside of the bra definitely didn't count!), reach "third base" (touching cunt), and score a "home run" (fucking). Here, six months later, I had made no progress. Oh, I'd stepped up the pressure on Kris: whenever we were making out, my hand would grope to her breasts. Usually she would quickly push my hand away. Sometimes, she'd let me leave it there for a moment, but only *outside* the sweater—"second base" was out of the question. In fact, a pissed off Kris had once asked, "Why do you keep *doing* that?" I didn't know what to say, so I just laughed nervously and said, "I don't know."

So, compared with my friends who were always talking about fucking and "eating pussy," I felt like a real rookie, stuck at first base. But it's not that I wasn't getting my rocks off regularly—in fact, I was jerking off every night, almost always while looking at pictures in the growing stack of *Playboy*, *Penthouse*, or *Oui* magazines I kept hidden under my bed. I liked to fixate on several different body parts of the naked or nearly naked models, but I increasingly liked to bring on my orgasm by fixating on that elusive "second base"—those bare, beautiful (and in real life, totally unavailable) female breasts.

One night, Will and I went to a local party of mostly high-school kids. Kris and I had temporarily broken up, and I was drunk on beer and feeling pretty confident, seeing as I was wearing my new leather-sleeved jacket with the letter H on it, which showed that I was a college man who had earned a letter on the local community-college basketball team. At one point, I found myself sitting on a bench talking with Sue, a high-school senior whom I'd seen around, but never spoken with. She was drinking, too, and we were soon making out right in the middle of the party. Excited, I suggested we go out to my car (actually my dad's three-quarter-ton Ford pickup truck). She surprised me by agreeing. Once in the truck, we began again to make out. I slid my hand under her sweater and slowly moved it toward her breast. Just as my fingertips touched her bra, she tugged firmly on my ear. Though I was drunk and nearly panting with sexual excitement, I knew that this was a clear signal that I should stop. So I did. Eventually, we said goodnight, but I asked her for a date the next Friday, and she agreed.

All that next week, I got psyched up. Part of the psyching up involved talking with Will about Sue. Will joked that Sue was a slut for having agreed to go out to my truck only a few minutes after having met me, and said that if I didn't succeed with her on Friday, I was "a total woos." I also got psyched up every night in private. As I jerked off, I imagined undoing Sue's bra (Will said it was easy and enjoyed demonstrating his method—"You just take your two hands and, 'click,' it comes apart") and being able to touch her bare breasts. She probably just stopped me the first time to protect her reputation, I thought to myself; on the second date, she definitely would want it.

Friday, I picked Sue up in the truck and took her to the drive-in movies. I had a couple of quarts of beer under the seat, but, to my disappointment, Sue declined to drink with me. I drank some anyway (she said she didn't mind), but not a whole lot. During the movie, I made my move. She was open to kissing, but was not nearly as passionate as she had been the previous week. I tried again to slip my hand inside her sweater, but once again pulled back when I got the old ear-pull. But I had my ace in the hole. My parents were out of town for the weekend, so I invited Sue to come to my house after the movie. She agreed, and I just knew that this meant she was willing to go further.

Once back at the house, I put on some music and again offered Sue some beer. She had a small glass, and I drank a bit more. Then we started making out on the couch. As we kissed, we both got more and more excited. Breathing heavily, we rolled on our sides, and Sue clinched my leg between her thighs. Ah-ha, I thought, I'm gonna get *at least* to second base here. Sitting upright again, I slipped both hands up the back of Sue's sweater. Her back felt smooth, and excited me, but I was going for the bra snaps. As my hands reached the middle of the back of her bra, Sue clenched her arms down on my arms, trying to slow or stop my attempt to undo her bra. Still kissing and breathing heavily, I continued to try to undo the bra. She was not cooperating with this effort, but wasn't saying anything either, and she continued to kiss me passionately. Due to my own inexperience and Sue's resistance, I could not get the damned bra undone. I kept trying to recall Will's simple instructions (I could even hear Will's "click" noise in my mind). I fumbled and twisted and pulled at the clasps in the back of the bra, all to no avail. To hell with the clasps, I thought, ever more excited. I moved my right hand around to the front of Sue's chest to her left breast. Just as my hand touched her breast, Sue tugged my ear. But my hand was *there*, dammit—I had a full head of steam and was sliding head-first into second base, and wasn't going to be stopped. So I quickly slipped my fingers under the elastic of the bra and pushed the bra up over her breast.

There was not a whole lot to the actual physical sensation of touching the breast. It felt very soft in my hand; I had expected it to be much firmer. But this moment was very, very brief, for just as I touched Sue's bare breast, I immediately ejaculated in my pants. Just as when I masturbated, the moment I came, my passion disappeared. But unlike when I masturbated, here I was, post-ejaculation, with my hand on the breast of a real, live person. What should I do next? I felt panic and embarrassment. Was she angry? Did she know I had come in my pants? I quickly withdrew my hand from inside her sweater, pulled away from her and mumbled, "Sorry." She fixed her bra and straightened her clothes and said, sarcastically, "Well! As long as you're *sorry*!" As quickly as possible, I retreated to the bathroom, and was pleased to find that my pants had contained most of the semen (it showed, but wasn't too obvious). I returned to the living room and suggested that I drive Sue home. She didn't disagree.

The next day, I told Will that I'd gotten to second base. But I didn't tell him any of the details and I certainly didn't feel proud. I never saw nor spoke to Sue again.

Part III

VIOLENCE, PAIN & INJURY

Every few years, *Sports Illustrated* runs a feature heralding the personalities and athletic exploits of linebackers. The most recent offering in this tradition appeared in the September 6, 1993 issue, in which linebackers were introduced as "search and destroy specialists whose taste for the punishing blow remains one of the game's few constants." Rick Telander, in a piece entitled "The Last Angry Men," described linebackers as "among the rare human beings who appreciate being called animals." Telander painted a picture of the linebacker's anger and thirst for mayhem as flowing from an instinctual pool of aggression. He quoted Chris Spielman, former inside linebacker for the Detroit Lions, who mused, "You are born with some type of aggressive streak in you." According to Telander's word processor-spun evolutionary theory, "Linebackers rise out of the football ooze in a curious twist on Darwin: While the primitive stayed below, groveling on all fours, the more primitive ascended to the upright position."

Readers are left with an impression of linebackers—and, by implication, men—as predestined by nature to be angry and violent. This is a false impression, however, because male aggression varies a great deal from individual to individual, within situations, and across cultures. Whether we're discussing fistfights in the stands or thumping on the field, the variations in men's propensity for violence are better explained by previous learning and social setting than by assumptions about innate biological drives.

Men's anger and violence derive, in part, from sexual inequality. Men use the threat or application of violence to maintain their political power and economic advantage over women. Male socialization reflects and reinforces this larger pattern of male dominance. As boys come to accept the male-dominated status quo, they internalize its concomitant cultural image of the angry and violence-prone prototypical man. Many male subcultures (such as athletic teams, fraternities, and gangs) are vehicles for transmitting these masculine norms, and, as such, do much to equate demonstrations of violence and anger with manhood.

Cross-cultural studies show that sexual segregation is linked to men's propensity for violence; that is, in societies with a lot of differences between men's and women's roles, outward displays of violence among men and in all-male settings are common. Similarly, studies of delinquent male gangs reveal that they have a subculture of violence. It may be that males in same-sex subcultures are more prone to exaggerate their physical strength in order to prove their manhood.

In U.S. culture, the linebacker embodies the aggressive, tough, masculine stereotype. The image of a linebacker is attractive to males; they find it useful as an ideal to separate themselves from women and to compare themselves to other men. Males commonly "size each other up" by gauging who is capable of beating up whom. When athletes or fans get "psyched" or "pumped up" before a game, part of what they are doing is drumming up anger inside themselves to draw on in attacking opponents. In some men, their anger gives them confidence that they are maintaining a strong, aggressive, independent, and fearless gender identity. In short, their anger is an emotional verification that they are successfully conforming to the dominant masculine stereotype.

Scratch a man, and very often he will bleed anger. Women wonder why men often get moody and periodically blow up like miniature psychosocial volcanoes. Men vent their anger on one another through fighting, ridicule, or cutthroat competition. Women are especially likely to be victimized by men's anger and violence, in the form of rape, wife-beating, assault, sexual harassment on the job, and verbal harassment. Women know that anger is a prerequisite for male violence. Most men, though they live with anger, have very little insight into its origins, presence, and movements within their bodies and minds.

We wrote this book to help men rethink and change their masculinity. We hope that, by thinking through aspects of men's violence in sports, men can gain insights into their anger and aggression outside sports—for example, in dating and marital relationships, friendships, politics, race relations, or war. The essays in this section are intended to be touchstones for rethinking and re-feeling the connections between sports, masculinity, and violence.

WHY ROCKY III?

MIKE MESSNER

I faithfully watched the first two. But I can't go see the third one. Not *Rocky III*. The Italian Stallion will have to go this final round without me.

Lately, I've been thinking more about boxing and enjoying it less. While watching the sports news on TV recently I saw a "promising young boxer" by the name of Dave Moore finishing off an opponent. I have never enjoyed watching a man being beaten into unconsciousness, but this particular instance was especially chilling. I felt as though I were seeing a ghost, for the fight brought back to me a song written by Bob Dylan in 1963 about a boxer of the same name, who was killed in the ring.* Dylan angrily asks several times through the song,

*In *Blood and Guts: Violence in Sports* (New York and London: Paddington Press, 1979; page 173), Don Atyeo tells the story of Davey Moore's last fight. In 1963, when Moore was featherweight champion, he was pounded in the ring by his opponent, Sugar Ramos. He died seventy-five hours later. A week after his death, three more boxers were killed in the ring, leading the Pope (among others) to call for the abolition of boxing.

Who killed Davey Moore?
Why did he die
And what's the reason for?

This question has plagued me for some time. Just who *is* responsible when a man is seriously injured or loses his life in the boxing ring? This issue was raised following last year's highly promoted championship bout between Sugar Ray Leonard and Thomas Hearns. Nearing the end of the fight, when Hearns was ahead on points, Leonard stung him with what was described as a "vicious combination of lefts and rights to the head" that left Hearns "dazed and staggering." The referee, who concluded that Hearns was "out on his feet," called the fight and awarded Leonard a technical knockout. Although the fight was applauded as a great one, some people were not so happy with its finish. For instance, the next day a young man commented to me that "the ref shouldn't have called the fight—you've gotta go down in a championship fight."

Indeed, boxing referees are caught in an extremely difficult bind. On the one hand, they are responsible for seeing that the fight ends before someone gets seriously injured. On the other hand, they face tremendous pressure from fans, promoters, television networks and sometimes the fighters themselves to let the fight go on until there is a clear-cut victory—until someone "goes down."

Not I, said the referee,
Don't point your little finger at me.
Sure, I coulda stopped it in the eighth
And saved him from his terrible fate.
But the crowd would have booed, I'm sure,
At not getting their money's worth.
Too bad that he had to go,
But there was pressure on me, too, you know.
No, it wasn't me that made him fall,
You can't blame me at all.

The need for a "clear decision" to end every boxing contest seems to be a growing problem. An earlier title fight between Leonard and Roberto Duran (the Animal, the Destroyer who had previously dethroned Leonard) was yet another example. After several hard-fought rounds, Duran was clearly being beaten. He was hurt, and was losing the ability to defend himself. Between rounds, he decided to quit, claiming that he had stomach cramps. He was soundly booed. The fans, who had paid large sums of money to witness what was promised to be a "monumental battle," were disappointed and angry. The criticism of Duran has not died down to this day. Some say he threw the fight. Most boxing fans seem to agree that when the chips were down, he was a "gutless quitter."

At about the same time that the Leonard-Duran fight was making news, I was following another story about the Welsh boxer Johnny Owen, who had been critically injured in a boxing match. "Owen Still in Coma" read the small blurbs—and, later, "Owen Dies." Like the mythological Rocky Balboa, Owen was a hard-working, ambitious young man from a poor, working-class background. He had said that his goal was to "fight a few more times and then get out of it before I get hurt." Certainly he was not a "gutless" man. He stayed in the fight to the end, undoubtedly pleasing the fans.

Not I, said the angry crowd,
Whose screams filled the arena loud
Too bad that he died that night,
But we just like to see a good fight
You can't blame us for his death,
We just like to see some sweat
There ain't nothing wrong in that
No, it wasn't us that made him fall,
You can't blame us at all.

Why do we fans push boxers to their limits, always demanding a clear-cut victory? This phenomenon can be seen as a result of a social-psychological malaise in modern life. Increasing instability and uncertainty in daily life, brought on by high unemployment, rising living costs, and increasingly shaky international relations (the United States, no longer the undisputed heavyweight champ, has been pushed around by relative lightweights like Iran), as well as insecure family relations and challenges to the traditional bases of masculinity, all bring about a need for *some* arena where there are obvious "good guys and bad guys"—clear winners and losers. For many people, sports has provided that arena. The National Football League has in recent years instituted a "fifth quarter" to decide games that end in a tie during regulation time. For players and for fans, it seems that "a tie is as good as a loss—it's like kissing your sister," as one fan told me.

Added to the fans' emotional investment is financial investment in boxing. Millions of dollars are bet on big matches. Fans pay hefty sums to watch the matches on cable television at home or on closed-circuit television in theaters. Like any other multimillion-dollar product on the market, boxing is heavily hyped by promoters and by the media. After all the hype and heavy betting preceding a match, a man can't just quit because he has stomach cramps. He's *gotta* go down.

Not I, says the boxing writer,
Pounding the print on his old typewriter.
Who says, boxing ain't to blame,
There's just as much danger in a football game.
Boxing is here to stay,
It's just the old American way.
No, you can't blame me at all,
It wasn't me that made him fall.

But what about the boxers themselves? What is it that made Sugar Ray Leonard return to the ring and risk losing the sight in an injured eye? As many would argue, the fighters know what they're getting into—they know the dangers. Of course, they also want the glory and the money that go with being on top. But those of us who watch boxing matches should ask some other questions. For instance, who are these men who risk life and limb for our entertainment? Most boxers are from poor, working-class backgrounds. Many are members of minority groups for whom boxing may seem to be one of the few ways out of the misery they were born into. According to Chris Dundee, a Miami boxing promoter, "Any man with a good trade isn't about to get knocked on his butt to make a dollar" (Atyeo 1979, 176-77). But an impoverished society (such as in many Latin American nations) or an economically depressed city (such as Detroit) is fertile ground for a flourishing boxing industry.

So even though nobody forces young boxers to enter the ring, it would be foolish to suggest that most of them freely choose boxing from a number of attractive alternatives. (Although many of the elite may romanticize the strength, stamina, courage, and masculinity of a John Wayne, we don't see many sons of the Rockefellers or the Kennedys taking up careers as pugilists, duking it out in the ring.) In any society which restricts the opportunities of certain groups of people, one will be able to find a significant number of those people who will be willing to pursue very dangerous careers for the slim chance of "making it big." Boxers are modern-day equivalents of Roman gladiators—they are both our victims and our heroes—and we are increasingly giving them the "thumbs down."

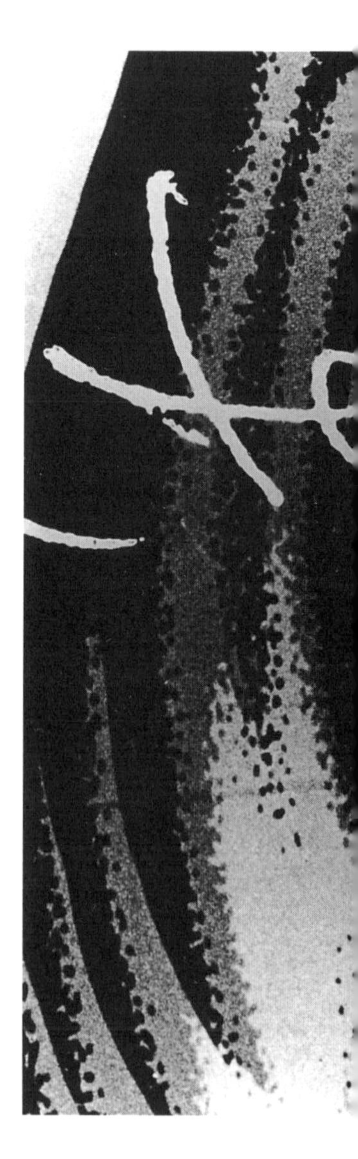

For every millionaire Ali and for every smiling Sugar Ray we see on our TV, there are hundreds of fighters who have never made enough money boxing even to

"Death of My Champion" by Andrew Uchin

live on. All they have received for their efforts are a few scattered cheers, some boos, and some permanent injuries. But to the fans they are mostly invisible—unless one of them has the impertinence to die in the ring. We just don't see the long-term damage a boxer takes from years of severe jolts to the internal organs and to the brain. According to J. A. N. Corsellis, a neurologist who has studied boxers and their injuries, "By the time a fighter has had even as few as 150 bouts, he is really, I think, very likely to have suffered brain damage" (Atyeo 1979, 182).

Does it make us wonder when we hear Muhammad Ali's once poetic and lightning-quick tongue, which used to "float like a butterfly," now often sticking to the roof of his mouth, as though it had been stung by a bee? And do we think about what boxing does to the people who watch the spectacle of boxing? Do we wonder to what extent boxing may serve to legitimate violence in everyday life?

Who killed Davey Moore?
Why did he die
And what's the reason for?

Dylan's question still troubles me. I think we can begin to find the answer by examining our own complicity in turning a brutal tradition into a profitable sport. The boxing business both meets the needs of an alienated and frustrated populace and at the same time generates millions of dollars for promoters, the media, and big-time betters. And part of the problem is in our society's conception of manhood. When the traditional bastions of masculinity are crumbling or being undermined by historical forces, few things are so affirming to the threatened male ego as a good boxing match. Boxing lets us feel our solidarity with other men as we vicariously express our repressed anger and violence.

When I was in junior high school, my friend Ron asked me to meet him after school because he was going to fight another boy and wanted some moral support. I watched as they fought. Ron's opponent was bigger, quicker and a better fighter. Before long, Ron was bleeding from the mouth. In a last-ditch effort, he let out a terrible scream and came at his opponent with a desperate and reckless windmill-like flailing of the arms. His pitiful attempt to take the offensive was answered with a stiff right to the nose that put him down on the ground, sobbing and humiliated. Two young men then showed up and broke up the fight. To my surprise, they did not say a thing to the two fighters, but, rather, they chastised those of us who had been watching and cheering the fighters on. "You're worse than those two," they told us. "Their fight would have ended before someone got hurt if you hadn't been here egging them on like you did. You should be ashamed of yourselves."

. . . and what's the reason for?

REFERENCE

Atyeo, Don. 1979. Blood and Guts: Violence in Sports. New York and London: Paddington Press.

Pigskin, Patriarchy and Pain

DON SABO

I am sitting down to write as I've done thousands of times over the past decade. But today there's something very different. I'm not in pain.

A half-year ago I underwent back surgery. My physician removed two disks from the lumbar region of my spine and fused three vertebrae using bone scrapings from my right hip. The surgery is called a "spinal fusion." For seventy-two hours I was completely immobilized. On the fifth day, I took a few faltering first steps with one of those aluminum walkers that are usually associated with elderly people in nursing homes. I progressed rapidly, and I left the hospital after nine days, completely free of pain for the first time in years.

How did I, once a well-intending and reasonably gentle boy from western Pennsylvania, ever get into so much pain? A simple explanation is I ended up in pain because I played a sport that brutalizes men's (and now sometimes women's) bodies. *Why* I played football and bit the bullet of pain, however, is more complicated. Like a young child who learns to dance or sing for a piece of candy, I played for rewards. Winning at sports meant winning friends and carving a place for myself within the male pecking order. Success at the game would make me less like myself and more like the older boys and my hero, Dick Butkus. Pictures of his hulking and snarling form filled my head and hung above my bed, beckoning me forward like a mythic Siren. If I could be like Butkus, I told myself, people would adore me as much as I adored him. I might even adore myself. As an adolescent, I hoped sports would get me attention from girls. Later, I became more practical-minded, and I worried about my future. What kind of work would I do for a living? Football became my ticket to a college scholarship, which in western Pennsylvania during the early sixties meant starting a career instead of getting stuck in the steel mills.

THE ROAD TO SURGERY

My bout with pain and spinal pathology began with a decision I made in 1955 when I was eight years old. I "went out" for football. At the time, I felt uncomfortable inside my body—too fat, too short, too weak. Freckles and glasses too! I wanted to change my image, and I felt that changing my body was one place to begin. My parents bought me a set of weights, and one of the older boys in the neighborhood was solicited to demonstrate their use. I can still remember the ease with which he lifted the barbell, the veins popping through his bulging biceps in the summer sun, and the sated look of strength and accomplishment on his face. This was to be the image of my future.

That fall I made a dinner-table announcement that I was going out for football. What followed was a rather inauspicious beginning. First, the initiation rites. Pricking the flesh with thorns until blood was drawn and having hot peppers rubbed in my eyes. Getting punched in the gut again and again. Being forced to wear a jockstrap around my nose and not knowing what was funny. Then came what was to be an endless series of proving myself: calisthenics until my arms ached; hitting hard and fast and knocking the other guy down; getting hit in the groin and not crying.

I "played" through grade school, co-captained my high school team, and went on to become an inside linebacker and defensive captain at the NCAA Division I level. I learned that pain and injury are "part of the game." I learned to be an animal. Coaches took notice of animals. Animals made first team. Being an animal meant being fanatically aggressive and ruthlessly competitive. If I saw an arm in front of me, I trampled it. Whenever blood was spilled, I nodded approval. The coaches taught me to "punish the other man," and to secretly see my opponents' broken bones as little victories within the bigger struggle. Little did I suspect, though, that I was devastating my own body at the same time. I endured broken noses, ribs, fingers, toes and teeth; torn muscles and ligaments; bruises, bad knees, and busted lips; and the gradual pulverizing of my spinal column, which, when I reached thirty and my jock career was long over, had caused seven years of near-constant pain. It was a long road to the surgeon's office.

Now surgically freed from the grip of pain, my understanding of pain has changed. Pain had gnawed away at my insides. Pain had turned my awareness inward. I had blamed myself for my predicament; I'd thought that I was solely responsible for every twinge and sleepless night. But this view was an illusion. My pain—each individual's pain—reflects an outer world of people, events, and forces.

The Pain Principle in football and other sports teaches boys and men that to endure pain is courageous, to survive pain is manly.

The origins of our pain are rooted *outside*, not inside, our skins.

THE PAIN PRINCIPLE

Sports are just one of many areas in our culture where pain is more important than pleasure. Boys are taught that to endure pain is courageous, to survive pain is manly. The principle that pain is good and pleasure is bad is plainly evident in the aphorism, so popular among coaches and athletes, "No pain, no gain." The pain principle affects the lives and psyches of male athletes in two fundamental ways. First, it stifles our awareness of our bodies and limits our emotional expression. Second, the pain principle encourages us to take the feelings that boil up inside us—feelings of insecurity and stress from striving so hard for success—and channel them into a bundle of rage that is directed at opponents. This posture toward oneself and the world is not limited to jocks. It is evident in the lives of many nonathletic men who, as "workaholics" or success-strivers or tough guys, deny their authentic physical and emotional needs and develop health problems as a result.

Today I no longer perceive myself as just an individual broken by athletic injury. Rather, I see myself as one man among many men who got swallowed up by a social system predicated on male domination. Patriarchy has two structural aspects. First, it is an hierarchical system in which men dominate women in sometimes crude and debasing, sometimes slick and subtle ways. Feminists have made great progress exposing and analyzing this side of the edifice of sexism. But patriarchy is also a system of intermale dominance, in which a minority of men dominates the masses of men. This intermale dominance hierarchy exploits the majority of those it beckons to climb its heights. Patriarchy's mythos of heroism and its morality of power-worship implant visions of masculine excellence and ecstasy in the minds of the boys who ultimately will defend its inequities and ridicule its victims. It is inside this institutional framework that I have begun to explore the essence and scope of the pain principle.

TAKING IT

Patriarchy is a form of social hierarchy. Hierarchy breeds inequity, and inequity breeds pain. To remain stable, the hierarchy must either justify the pain or explain it away. In patriarchy, women and the masses of men learn that pain is inevitable and that it enhances one's character and moral worth. This principle is expressed in Judeo-Christian beliefs. The Judeo-Christian god inflicts or permits pain, yet "the Father" is still revered and loved. Likewise, as chief disciplinarian in the patriarchal family, the father has the right to inflict pain. The pain principle also echoes throughout traditional Western sexual morality: it is better to experience the pain of *not* having sexual pleasure than it is to have sexual pleasure.

Most men learn to heed these cultural messages and take their cues for survival from the patriarchy. The Willie Lomans of the economy pander to the prophets of profit and the American Dream. Soldiers, young and old, salute their neo-Hun generals. Right-wing Christians genuflect before the idols of righteousness, affluence, and conformity. And male athletes adopt the visions and values that coaches are offering: to take orders, to take pain, to "take out" opponents, to take the game seriously, to take women, and to take their place on the team. And if the athletes can't "take it," they lose the rewards of athletic camaraderie, prestige, scholarships, pro contracts, and community recognition.

Becoming a football player fosters conformity to male-chauvinistic values and self-abusing lifestyles. It contributes to the legitimacy of a social structure based on patriarchal power. When men compete for prestige and status in sports (or elsewhere), they identify with the relatively few males who control resources and are able to bestow rewards and inflict punishment. Male supremacists are not born, they are made, and traditional athletic socialization is a fundamental contribution to this complex social-psychological and political process. Through sports, many males, indeed, learn to "take it"—that is, to internalize patriarchal values, to incorporate these values in their gender identity and in their views of women and society.

My high-school coach once evoked the pain principle during a pre-game pep talk. For what seemed an eternity, he paced frenetically and silently before us with fists clenched and head bowed. He suddenly stopped and faced us with a smile. It was as though he had approached a podium to begin a long-awaited lecture. "Boys," he began, "people who say football is a 'contact sport' are dead wrong. Dancing is a contact sport. Football is a game of pain and violence! Now get the hell out of here and kick some ass." Surging in unison to fight the coach's war, we practically ran through the wall leaving the locker room. I see now that the coach was right but for all the wrong reasons. I should have taken him at his word and never played the game.

When Bodies Are Weapons

MIKE MESSNER

In many of our most popular spectator sports, winning depends on the use of violence. To score and win, the human body is routinely turned into a weapon to be used against other bodies, causing pain, serious injury, and even death. How do we interpret the social meaning of this violence? Is it socially learned behavior that serves to legitimize masculine power over women? Commentators—both apologists and critics—have made sweeping statements about sports and violence, but their analyses rarely take into account the meanings of violence in sports to the athletes themselves. We can begin to understand the broader social meanings of violence in sports by listening to the words of former athletes.

With the possible exception of the boxer in the ring, perhaps the one position in modern sports that requires the most constant physical aggressiveness is that of lineman in U.S. football. While TV cameras focus primarily on those few who carry, throw, catch, and kick the ball, the majority of the players on the field are lined up a few inches apart from each other. On each play they snarl, grunt, and curse; at the snap of the ball they slam their large and heavily armored bodies into each other. Blood, bruises, broken bones, and concussions often result.

Marvin Upshaw, now thirty-six years old, was a lineman in professional football for nine years. He seemed a bit stung when I asked him how he could submit to such punishment for so many years:

> You know, a lot of people look at a lineman and they say, "Oh, man, you gotta be some kinda *animal* to get down there and beat on each other like that." But it's just like a woman giving birth. Everybody says, you know, "That's a great accomplishment; she must be really beautiful." And I do, too—I think it's something that's an act of God, that's unreal. But she hasn't done nothing that she wasn't *built* for. See what I'm saying? Now here I am, 260, 270 pounds, and that's my position. My physical self helped me. . . . That's what I'm built for. Just like a truck carrying a big Caterpillar: you see the strain, but that's what it's built for. So as far as that being a real big accomplishment, it is, but it's not. That's all you were built for.

BORN OR BUILT?

Upshaw's comparisons of the aggressive uses of his body in football with a woman giving birth and with a truck are telling. These comparisons exemplify one of the major paradoxes in men's construction of meaning surrounding the use of their bodies as weapons. On the one hand, many of the men I interviewed explained their aggression and violence as natural: to them, repeated bone-crunching collisions with other men are simply "an act of God," "like a woman giving birth." On the other hand, they know that their bodies are, like trucks, "built" by human beings to do a specific job. Time after time I have heard former athletes, almost in the same breath, talk of their "natural" and

"God-given" talent *and* of the long hours, days, and years of training and sacrifice that went into developing their bodies and their skills. "I was a natural," said MacArthur Lane, a former professional football star. "Just about every hour of the day when I wasn't sleeping or eating, I'd be on the playground competing."

Similarly, Jack Tatum, who in his years with the Oakland Raiders was known as the Assassin for his fierce and violent "hits" on opposing receivers, described himself as a "natural hitter." But his descriptions of his earliest experiences in high school football tell a different story. Though he soon began to develop a reputation as a fierce defensive back, hitting people bothered him at first:

> When I first started playing, if I would hit a guy hard and he wouldn't get up, it would bother me. [But] when I was a sophomore in high school, first game, I knocked out two quarterbacks, and people loved it. The coach loved it. The more you play, the more you realize that it is just a part of the game—somebody's gonna get hurt. It could be you, it could be him—most of the time it's better if it's him.

Tatum's words suggest that the routine use of violence against others to achieve an athletic goal doesn't come naturally at all, but may require a good deal of encouragement from others. Recent studies of young ice hockey players corroborate this: the combination of violent adult athletic role models and rewards from coaches, peers, and the community for the willingness to successfully use violence creates a context in which violence becomes normative behavior. Young males who earn reputations as aggressive "hitters" often gain a certain status in the community and among their peers, thus anchoring (at least temporarily) what otherwise might be insecure masculine identities.

TWO INFAMOUS "HITS"

What happens when legitimate ("legal") aggression results in serious injury, as it so often does in sports? Both Jack Tatum and Ray

Fosse, a former professional baseball player, were involved in frighteningly violent collisions, each of which resulted in serious injury. In each incident, the play was "legal"—no penalty was issued by officials. Each incident also stimulated a lively public controversy concerning violence in sports. These two men's remembrances are instructive in connecting the athlete's experiences of violence in sports with the larger social meanings surrounding such public incidents.

By the time Jack Tatum got to the pros, he had become the kind of fearsome hitter that coaches dream of. Though he took pride in the fact that he was not a "dirty" player (i.e., his hits were within the rules), he was perhaps too good at his craft. Intimidation was the name of the game, but there was growing concern within football and in the sports media that Jack Tatum's "knockouts" were too brutal. In 1978, Tatum delivered one of his hits to an opposing wide receiver, Darryl Stingley. Stingley's neck was broken in two places, and he would never walk again. Suddenly, Tatum was labeled as part of a "criminal element" in the National Football League. Tatum was confused, arguing that this had been a "terrible accident," but was nevertheless simply a "routine play" which was "within the rules."

> I guess the thing that mystified me was that I could play for nine years and one guy gets hurt and then everybody comes down on me, you know. It's just like for nine years I've been playing the game the wrong way. But I've made All-Pro, I've been runner-up for Rookie of the Year, I've got all the honors playing exactly the same way. So, you know, it just kind of mystified me as to why there was just all of a sudden this stuff because a guy got hurt. It wasn't the first time a guy got paralyzed in football, so it really wasn't that unusual.

Ray Fosse received a violent hit from Pete Rose in the 1970 Major League Baseball All-Star game, while 60 million people watched on television. In the twelfth inning, Pete Rose was steaming around third base; he needed only to touch home plate in order to score the winning

Popular culture and sports media tend to glorify the violent use of the male body in sports. A normal result of combat sports is that each year thousands of athletes incur serious and permanent injuries.

run. Fosse's job as catcher was to block the plate with his body and hope that the ball arrived in time for him to catch it and tag Rose out. Rose arrived a split second before the ball, and, looking a lot like a football player delivering a hit, drove his body straight at Fosse and touched the plate safely. Fosse's shoulder was separated, and despite his youth he never fully regained the powerful home-run swing he had demonstrated earlier that summer. Again, a serious injury had resulted from a technically legal play. Rose was seen by some as a hero, but others criticized him, asking if it was right for him to hurt someone else simply to score a run in what was essentially an exhibition game. Rose seemed as mystified by these questions as Jack Tatum had been. "I play to win," responded Rose. "I just did what I had to do."

When I interviewed Fosse years later, well into his retirement, he lamented the effect of the injury but saw it not as the result of a decision by Pete Rose but rather as "part of the game." It was fate that had broken his body—not a person. In fact, he felt nothing but respect for Rose:

> I never once believed that he hit me intentionally. He's just a competitor, and I only wish that every other major-league ball player played as hard as he did. . . . But I would say that that was the beginning of a lot of pain and problems for me. . . .

There is clearly a contextual morality in Tatum's and Fosse's constructions of meaning surrounding these two violent collisions. The rules of the game provide a context that frees the participants from the responsibility for moral choices. As long as the participants play by the rules, they not only feel that they should be free from moral criticism, but also understand that they are entitled to "respect"—that form of emotionally distant connection with others that is so important to traditional masculine identity. Flagrant rule-violators, most athletes believe, are "violent" and deserve to be penalized; others, like Tatum and Rose, are "aggressive competitors" deserving of respect. But this distinction is shaken when serious injury results from "legal" actions, and public scrutiny raises questions about the athletes' personal morality. Both

Tatum and Fosse appear mystified by the public perspective on events in terms of individual choice or morality. They just play by the rules.

THE PRICE ATHLETES PLAY

There is another painful paradox in today's organized combat sports. Top athletes, who are popularly portrayed as models of good physical conditioning and health, suffer from a very high incidence of permanent injuries, alcoholism, drug abuse, obesity, and heart problems when they retire. The way athletes are taught to regard their bodies as machines and weapons with which to annihilate opponents often results in their using violence against their own bodies. Partly for this reason, former professional football players in the United States have an average life-expectancy of about fifty-six years—roughly fifteen years shorter than the overall average life-expectancy of U.S. males. Football, of course, is especially brutal, but baseball has had its share of casualties, too. Ray Fosse's interview with me seemed to be an almost endless chronicle of injuries and surgeries. "When someone got injured," he explained, "we had a saying: 'Throw dirt on it, spit on it, go play'."

Not only professional athletes parade their injuries this way. Nearly every former athlete I interviewed, amateur or professional, told at least one story of an injury that disabled him, at least for a time. Many had incurred serious injuries that had permanently harmed their health. Although most wore these injuries with pride, like badges of masculine status, athletes also grudgingly acknowledged that their healthy bodies were a heavy price to pay for glory. But for them to question their decisions to "give up" their bodies would ultimately mean questioning the entire system of rules through which they had successfully established relationships and a sense of identity. Instead, former athletes usually rationalized their own injuries as "part of the game." They claimed that their pain contributed to the development of their character and ultimately gained them the respect of others.

Clearly, heavy personal costs are paid by those who participate in violent organized sports. And, because of poverty, institutionalized racism and lack of other career options, it is poor and ethnic minority males who are disproportionately channeled into athletic careers—and especially into the more dangerous positions within the combat sports. Males from more privileged backgrounds often play sports in school, but because they face a wider range of educational and career choices they often choose to leave sports at a relatively early age. Young men from poor and non-white backgrounds face a constricted range of options. Lacking other resources and choices, they may see sports as the one legitimate context in which a youngster from a disadvantaged background can establish a sense of masculine identity in the world.

SPORTS VIOLENCE AND GENDER RELATIONS

With the twentieth century decline in the practical need for physical strength in work and in warfare, representations of the muscular male body as strong, virile, and powerful have taken on increasingly important ideological significance in gender relations. Indeed, the body plays such a central role in the construction of contemporary gender relations because it is so closely associated with the natural. Yet, to develop their bodies for competition, athletes spend a tremendous amount of time exercising and weight-training, and sometimes even use illegal and dangerous drugs, such as steroids. Though an athletic body is popularly thought of as natural, it is nevertheless the product of social practice.

The embodiment of culturally dominant forms of masculinity entails the imbedding of force and skill in the body. Through this process, men's power over women comes to appear as though it is natural. Sports are an important organizing institution for the embodiment of dominant masculinity. Sports suppress natural (sex) similarities, construct differences, and then, largely through the media, weave a structure of symbol and interpretation around these differences which naturalizes them. Several theorists have suggested that the major ideological salience of sports as mediated spectacle may lie not so much in violence as it does in the opportunity sports give male spectators to identify with the muscular male body. Morse, in a fascinating analysis of the use of slow-motion instant replays in football, argues that the visual representation of violence is transformed by slow motion replays into gracefulness (Morse 1983). The salient social meanings of these images of male power

After being rewarded by coaches, peers and fans for the successful utilization of violence, football players come to view the constant pain and the possibility of serious injury as "part of the game."

and grace lie not in identification with violence, Morse argues, but rather, in narcissistic and homoerotic identification with the male body. Perhaps the violence represents a denial of the homoeroticism in sports.

Violence in sports may play another important social role—that of constructing differences among men. Whereas males from lower socioeconomic and ethnic minority backgrounds disproportionately pursue careers in violent sports, privileged men are likelier, as Woody Guthrie once suggested, to commit violence against others "with fountain pens." But with the exception of domestic violence against women and children, physical violence is rarely a part of the everyday lives of these men. Yet violence among men may still have important ideological and psychological meaning for men from privileged backgrounds. There is a curious preoccupation among middle-class males with both movie characters who are working-class tough guys, and with athletes who are fearsome "hitters" and who heroically "play hurt." These tough guys of the culture industry are both heroes, who "prove" that "we men" are superior to women, and the "other" against whom privileged men define themselves as "modern." The "tough guys" are, in a sense, contemporary gladiators sacrificed so that elite men can have a clear sense of where they stand in the intermale pecking order. Ironically, although many young black males are attracted to sports as a milieu in which they can find respect, to succeed in sports they must become intimidating, aggressive, and violent. Television images—like that of Jack Tatum "exploding" Darryl Stingley—become symbolic "proof" of the racist belief that black males are naturally more violent and aggressive. Their marginalization as men—signified by their engaging in the very violence that makes them such attractive spectacles—contributes to the construction of culturally dominant (white, upper- and middle-class) masculinity.

REFERENCE

Morse, M. 1983. "Sport on Television: Replay and Display," pp. 44-66. In *Regarding Television: Critical Approaches*, ed. E. A. Kaplan. Los Angeles: University Publications of America.

Part IV

GAY ATHLETES AND HOMOPHOBIA

After emerging on the North American scene in the late 1960s, the gay-rights movement ushered in an era of intense debate and political struggle. A recent poll by U.S. News and World Report (July 5, 1993) showed that American voters are painfully ambivalent about lesbian and gay issues. While 65 percent of 1,000 persons polled indicated they believed in equal rights for gay people, most regarded homosexuality as a lifestyle choice, and half opposed extending civil-rights laws to include gays and lesbians. Fifty-three percent said that they actually knew a gay man or lesbian, and that this relationship made them feel better about gay rights in general. Still, 60 percent opposed "legal partnerships" for homosexuals, while only 35 percent approved the idea. Only 24 percent felt that gays and lesbians should be allowed to adopt children, and 70 percent opposed this view.

Today the debate over gay rights is being waged in a variety of institutions, including government, religion, the military, and, more recently, sports. Several factors have spurred public discussion of homosexuality in sports. First, women in sports have always battled those who use the accusation of lesbianism to belittle women's athletic performances or undercut women's chances of moving up in coaching and sports administration careers. Second, a number of retired male athletes—such as Dave Kopay (a pro-football player), Dave Pallone (a pro-baseball umpire), Bruce Hayes (an Olympic swimmer), Glenn Burke (of the Los Angeles Dodgers), and Tom Waddell (an Olympic decathlete)—have come out of the locker room closet, and Martina Navratilova, the tennis superstar, has long been courageously outspoken about her lesbianism. The sports media have treated these cases with great interest. Third, although there have always been some homosexual athletes, recently the number of openly gay and lesbian athletes seems to be increasing. The Gay Games, for example, attract between ten thousand and fifteen thousand participants. A proportion of athletes have always been gay but, because coming out brings particularly heavy stigma in the heterosexist world of sport, most remain in the closet.

Feelings about gay issues in sports run so deep because homophobia—irrational fear or hatred of gay men, lesbians, and bisexuals—is so prevalent. You know you're homophobic if you get anxious and afraid when you think you may be perceived as gay or lesbian by others. Becoming anxious or repulsed when you find yourself attracted to a person of your own sex, or being afraid that you have homo- or bisexual tendencies, are also signs of homophobia. Homophobic thoughts and feelings are a pervasive part of our culture and gender politics.

The articles in this section focus on homophobia's effects on the personal experiences of both straight and gay athletes, and on the connections between homophobia, sexism, and structured sexual inequality in sports. The essays are intended to raise questions, and, in the process, to create a better understanding of the links between sports, masculinity, and society.

The Politics of Homophobia in Sport

DON SABO

Bill Clinton, newly elected president, created a minor furor in 1993 when he recommended open acceptance of gays and lesbians in the military. Pentagon officials lined up in front of microphones and congressional office doors to express their concerns about morale, morality, and American military preparedness. Gen. "Stormin' Norman" Schwartzkopf, the Persian Gulf war hero, publicly opposed Clinton's directive, and there were signs that Gen. Colin Powell might resign as head of the Joint Chiefs of Staff. Opposition also came from conservative political lobbies, religious groups, and veterans organizations. Besides challenging the military policy of exclusion based on sexual orientation, the Clinton directive ruptured decades of silence around gay and lesbian life in the military. As the silence was broken, heterosexism and homophobia were shown to be as much a part of the military landscape as boot camp, uniforms, and war games.

Sports is another institution in which homophobia has been an integral strand in the web of group relations. Though athletics have always had homosexual participants, open discussion of their experiences or rights has been taboo. It was not until the 1980s, for example, that sport scientists, physical educators, and athletic administrators began to formally discuss homophobia in their conferences. Beneath the canopy of formal silence around gay issues in sports, however, has always been plenty of informal references to gays and lesbians, jokes about effeminate men and mannish women, subtle accusations involving sexual preference, discriminatory practices, and sometimes even physical harassment of gays and lesbians.

Like other forms of prejudice, homophobia feeds on stereotypes and promotes unfair discrimination. Key to the controversy surrounding gays and lesbians in sports is the potential of homosexuality to undermine institutionalized male dominance and sexist beliefs. Ironically, many so-called gay issues in sport are more fundamentally gender issues and sex equality issues.

LEARNING HOMOPHOBIC MASCULINITY

I was recently the guest speaker at an athletic banquet at a parochial middle school. Parents, grandparents, coaches, school administrators, and young athletes had gathered together in the church-basement cafeteria to celebrate their athletic dreams and achievements. The kids, who ranged from the fourth through the eighth grades, were absolutely beautiful, and the room seemed to almost tilt back and forth from the force of their collective energy. The room hushed, however, as they filed up one by one to receive accolades and laminated plastic trophies that were, in their sparkling eyes, as good as gold.

After the awards ceremony, a father of a fourth-grade boy told me that his son had been called a lesbian by a friend. His son had replied indignantly, "I can't be a lesbian, stupid. You have to be a girl to be a lesbian." The anecdote illustrates two lessons about how homophobia filters into a boy's developing identity. First, males are not born homophobes, they gradually learn homophobic sentiments and ideas as they grow up. In his study of racial and ethnic intolerance,

Gordon Allport, a psychologist, described how children learn prejudice from their parents. At first, during the "pre-linguistic phase," children sense rather than know that their parents regard some people as being different and inferior. In this phase, prejudice mainly takes the form of feelings and only vague perceptions of the inferiorized and despised group (such as blacks, Puerto Ricans, or Jews). To show how this early prejudicial awareness operates, Allport tells the story of the little girl who ran home from play to ask, "Mommy, what is the name of the people I'm supposed to hate?" In later stages, of course, children learn more details about the despised group, stereotyped images take form in their minds, and once fleeting negative sentiments become permanent psychic fixtures. Prejudice against homosexuals may develop in the same way.

Second, the flowering of homophobic beliefs and emotions in young males is intricately tied to their development of gender identity. While growing up, boys internalize various cultural messages about masculinity. They learn to behave "like men," which means not to behave like women. They are told—don't be a sissy or a wimp. Keep a stiff upper lip. Big boys don't cry. Take it like a man. Be independent; try not to depend on others. Be tough and aggressive, and keep your feelings to yourself. Homophobia is yet another message sent to boys across the American cultural air waves. This message says that, like oil and water, homosexuality and masculinity do not mix. As boys begin to view homosexuality as a "negation of masculinity," as Bob Connell (1992, 736) puts it, they come to equate homophobia with masculinity. Gregory Herek (1986, 563) explains that "to be 'a man' in contemporary American society is to be homophobic—that is, to be hostile toward homosexual persons in general and gay men in particular."

In athletics, the lessons of homophobia are learned and acted out in various ways, of which teasing and ridiculing are probably the most common. The razzing and joking that go on in most locker rooms communicate that homosexuals are inferior, silly, sick, or disgusting. The terms fag and faggot may be used to mock, insult, or aggravate a teammate. Lack of toughness, open displays of sympathy, or other behavior that is considered feminine might also provoke ridicule.

Some coaches use homophobia as a motivational device. Playing on the gender and sexual insecurities of adolescent athletes, coaches use the threat of homosexual stigmatization to muster allegiance to themselves or esprit d'corps among the ranks. Such ploys work because they reflect and feed the anti-gay sentiment that already exists in the locker-room subculture. An incident I remember from a high-school football practice illustrates this dynamic. A sophomore named Brian, a big lug but rather flabby, lacked the physical strength and the "killer instinct" that we were taught to believe was necessary to be a good player. One hot August afternoon, Coach "Sleepy Joe" Shumock decided to teach poor Brian "how to block, once and for all." He lined up the entire defensive team and made Brian block each one of us, one after the other. All the while, Coach taunted him:

> How many sisters you got at home, Brian? Is it six or seven? How long did it take your mother to find out you were a boy, Brian? When did you stop wearing dresses like your sisters, Brian? Maybe Brian would like to bake cookies for us tomorrow, boys. You're soft, Brian, maybe too soft for this team. What do you think, boys, is Brian too soft for the team?

The ordeal went on for at least ten minutes, until Brian collapsed, exhausted and in tears. Coach had won. I felt sorry for Brian; he may not have been "an animal" or a good player, but he was out there sweating and beating himself up with the rest of us. I realized, though, that being "soft" was to be avoided at all costs. I ultimately sided with the coach and the "team." I identified "up" the male hierarchy in solidarity with the team rather than "down" with Brian's vulnerability and suffering. I now understand that the coach's onslaught of homophobic messages stayed with me long after Brian's tears had dried in the August heat.

The "homophobe persona" is another vehicle through which homophobia gets translated into social action. Some young men act out the role of a gay-hater as a way of constructing their manly identity and building a reputation among their male peers. They usually do this by publicly ridiculing gay men, but they may also physically confront gays. Gay-bashing, the physical beating, even killing, of gays, is an extreme form of this behavior. Gay-haters' conscious or unconscious strategy is to become the "big man on campus" by being the big homophobe on campus. Teammates or fraternity brothers in effect become the audience to which the homophobe plays out the theme "I am a real man because I hate gays" or "I'll prove I'm heterosexual by hassling gays and lesbians." The belief that some sports are inherently more masculine than others also promotes homophobia among athletes. Jim Estep, a college professor and a former captain of the U.S. Naval Academy fencing team, recalled that whereas "football, basketball, and lacrosse were considered macho sports, fencing was looked down upon as being effeminate. There was the added inference that, if fencing was effeminate, then the participants in it might be gay."

This belief was communicated among students, Jim knew, even though nobody ever actually accused him or his teammates of being a homosexual. Once, when it was announced at the evening meal that Jim had earned second place in an eastern United States intercollegiate fencing tournament, some of the men at his table hooted and waved limp wrists in his face. And at the regular meetings of team captains from various sports, those from the more prestigious "macho" sports ignored him.

> My voice wasn't heard. My sport was viewed as less important and less macho than theirs. In their minds, football and basketball were about masculine traits like size, strength, and force. Fencing, in contrast, was more about strategy and subtlety, and these traits were considered feminine and inferior.

The manifestations of homophobia in sports can be very subtle. I have wondered, for example, why male gymnasts do not use music in their floor exercises while female gymnasts do. Whereas the lack of music in men's floor exercise seems to accentuate the gymnasts' muscular strength, the presence of music in women's floor exercise seems to sidetrack recognition of the strength and muscle that they bring to gymnastics. Is men's gracefulness in floor exercise deemphasized because it transgresses against the code of homophobic masculinity? Is female gymnasts' gracefulness exaggerated to conform to stereotypical notions of femininity?

In summary, homophobia is not inborn but learned. As a boy grows up, homophobic sentiments and attitudes become grafted to his developing personality and gender identity. A boy's inner sense of manliness develops in juxtaposition to his sense of what it means to be gay or feminine. And yet, there is more to homophobia than sexual preference or conformity to gender stereotypes. Like other forms of prejudice, homophobia gets acted out and perpetuated in our relationships with other people. Homophobia derives from and reinforces a wide range of power relations among individuals and groups. These relations, in turn, are tied to systems of inequality.

THE POLITICS OF HOMOPHOBIA

Gays and lesbians face a constant threat of stigma and discrimination. Compared to the civil rights enjoyed by the heterosexual majority, the political voice and freedoms of the homosexual minority are extremely limited. The public sees the politics of gay rights as being strictly related to homosexual interests alone. This view, however, is misguided and narrow.

Politics are about power. Power concerns the ability of one person or group to impose its will on another group with or without its consent

Homophobia in sports tends to limit both women's and men's perceptions of their potential options for growth and expression.

or collaboration. Homophobia is political because it enters into the web of power relations between straights and gays, men and women, and groups of men within the intermale dominance hierarchies that make up contemporary gender relations.

In a male-dominated social order, men generally monopolize power, status, and resources. Women, in contrast, have less access to power and social rewards. Within each institution in the male-dominated society, gender roles are defined in ways that tend to insure social and political dominance for men and secondary social status for women. By adhering to traditional gender roles, therefore, men and women meet the requirements of the larger system of sexual inequality. If many individuals or groups were to abandon traditional gender roles, patriarchal institutions would be forced to change, and the disparities of power and privilege between men and women might be lessened. This is precisely where homophobia enters the picture. Homophobia serves as a vehicle for social control by making conformity to traditional gender expectations desirable and nonconformity something to be feared and disdained.

Lehne (1989) argues that homophobia enforces the rigid sex roles of *both gay and straight* men. The threat of being labeled feminine, a faggot, or a sissy may be used by football coaches, fathers, peers, or psychiatrists to pressure men to conform to traditional gender expectations in a variety of social situations. As long as men and women, whether they are heterosexual or homosexual, conform to traditional gender expectations, they help to maintain the social and political dominance of elite males. As Lehne (1989: 419) writes, "Since males control power in our society, and use this power for their own benefit, people who may not support the dominant male role are excluded from positions of power because of the possibility they will not use this power to further male interests."

HOMOPHOBIA, ATHLETICS, AND GENDER

A few basic questions can help uncover the politics of homophobia in sports. Who benefits from homophobia in sport? Who is empowered by homophobia, and who is handcuffed by it?

Homophobia reinforces sexual inequality and male hegemony in sports in several ways. First, homophobia obviously hurts gay athletes, who face the daily threat of stigma and discrimination (Lenskyj 1986). A young gay male may quit the basketball team because he is afraid of being found out or just tired of listening to the anti-gay talk. A female basketball player who openly identifies herself as a lesbian or, perhaps, is suspected of being a lesbian, may be ridiculed or ostracized by peers.

Second, homophobia serves to enforce conformity to traditional gender roles, thereby reinforcing male hegemony. For example, the threat of being labeled a homosexual forces boys and men to behave in accordance with traditional masculine stereotypes. A young male who takes an interest in any nonsexual but culturally defined feminine activity such as dance or nursing, is often considered queer and labeled a sissy or faggot. The girl interested in playing contact sports gets snickers from boys and cold shoulders from girls. The threat of homosexual stigma, therefore, serves primarily to maintain gender stereotypes and only secondarily as a vehicle for regulating sexual behavior. Hence, *both* gay and straight athletes are hurt by constrictive gender stereotypes (Lenskyj 1986; Griffin 1991).

Third, homophobia promotes the cultural devaluation of women. A gay male, or a "fag," is regarded as an effeminate man, or one who thinks, acts, or feels like a woman. To call a man effeminate probably wouldn't be insulting if women weren't considered inferior to men. In contrast, many men perceive lesbians to be women acting like men.

Though lesbian athletes in sport have been maligned and mistreated, gay athletes have been generally subject to more vigorous silencing and stigmatization. David Kopay, for ten years a star running back in the National Football League, created a sensation when he became the first gay jock to come out of the closet in the 1970s. Kopay was subsequently banished from the National Football League and could not find other employment in sports (Kopay and Young 1977). One possible explanation for the harsher treatment of male than female homosexuals is that gay men represent a more serious challenge to the political dominance of male elites than lesbians. Marilyn French (1985) has observed that patriarchy arose so male elites could subjugate not only women, but also lesser-status males. Homophobia helps maintain the dominance of elite males because it fosters conformity to hegemonic masculinity *within* male dominance hierarchies at the same time that it degrades women and femininity. Some closeted gay male athletes realize that they have a lot to lose by "coming out"; as long as they stay "in the closet," they can still share the benefits of hegemonic masculinity. Female athletes, who are already in subordinate positions, may have less to lose by breaking silences.

There is another reason that lesbians may be tolerated a bit more in sports than gay men. Men perceive lesbians as basically emulating men. This belief is expressed in men's pornographic portrayals of lesbian love, in which dildoes, symbolizing penises, occupy center-stage. Portraying lesbians with dildoes belittles the concept of women loving women. Lesbianism is thus recast by heterosexist culture as an emulation of masculinity. In contrast, male homosexuality is considered a negation of masculinity. Somehow, it is a less grievous breach of the cultural codes surrounding hegemonic masculinity for women not to love and need men than it is for men not to love and need masculinity.

Fourth, homophobia in sports hurts even women who aren't lesbians. Allegations of lesbianism and questions about women's sexual preferences are sometimes used on college and university campuses to intimidate female students and faculty members. Female coaches and athletic administrators are especially vulnerable to such rumor and innuendo. What is going on here? Is it that male coaches and athletic administrators are anxious about the "femininity" of their female colleagues? Not likely. Within the male-dominated hierarchy of sports, men hold most of the prestige, power, and resources. Accusations that playing sports "masculinizes" women, or that female leaders are lesbians, serve to discredit both straight and homosexual female athletes so that men can retain their higher status and control of resources.

Finally, the moralizing and policing carried on to discourage homosexuality among athletes distract public awareness from heterosexual misconduct in sports. Male coaches' sexual abuse of female athletes is ignored, despite much anecdotal evidence for its prevalence. And, until recently, the homophobia in organized men's sports has hidden the connections between locker-room sexism and the sexual maltreatment of women outside sports.

UNLEARNING HOMOPHOBIC MASCULINITY

What can be gained from getting rid of homophobia in sports? Athletics would become a more hospitable environment for gays and lesbians, and we might all forget some of the sexist myths that surround sports such as—

- Sports are for men and not for women.
- All male softball players are heterosexual, whereas all female softball players are lesbians.
- Gay men are delicate and nonathletic, whereas straight men are tough, strong, and athletic.
- Homophobia is normal and healthy.

As men climb out from under some of the timeworn sexist myths associated with sports, they might discover greater levels of athletic freedom and expression. As one former college basketball player discovered,

> I know of some very good volleyball players, who are among the best in North America, who are very effeminate, drag-queen types, and that opened my eyes a long time ago. How could this person possibly be better than me when they have long hair, long fingernails, every time he gets a spike he screams, and then I realized that your level of masculinity or femininity doesn't have a hell of a lot to do with your athletic ability. (Pronger 1990)

Would open acceptance of gay men in athletics mean that heterosexual males would be sexually harassed in the locker room? This concern has been articulated in congressional hearings on gays in the military. The charge is that heterosexual men would be ogled and subjected to unwanted sexual advances in the showers if gays were openly accepted into the military ranks. Such concerns seem unrealistic. Gay men seldom come on to straight men. Instead, gay men usually gravitate toward one another in the same way that heterosexual men generally seek out women as potential partners. As far as ogling goes, any man who has spent time in a locker room knows that virtually all men sometimes look at one another's genitals. Finally, there is a deep irony in straight men's fears about being hit on by gay men in that heterosexual men have been hitting on women in various ways (ranging from crude to sophisticated) for centuries.

Homophobia is a complicated issue in sports, as it is in other institutions, such as the military, organized religion, and education. Homophobia in sports limits the ability of individuals to pursue a crucial athletic value—that each individual can become everything that she or he is capable of being. Furthermore, sports themselves are limited by homophobia; it prevents sports from being a more inclusive place for children and adults to grow. Inside and outside of sports, homophobia is a moat that must be crossed if we are going to create institutions and relationships based on equality and tolerance.

REFERENCES

Connell, R. W. 1992. "A Very Straight Gay: Masculinity, Homosexual Experience, and the Dynamics of Gender." *American Sociological Review* 57(6):735-51.

French, M. 1985. *Beyond Power*. New York: Ballantine Books.

Griffin, P. 1991. Silence Encourages Fear, Discrimination. *USA Today*, September 18.

Herek, G. M. 1986. "On Heterosexual Masculinity: Some Psychical Consequences of the Social Construction of Gender and Sexuality." *American Behavioral Scientist* 29:563-77.

Kopay, D., and P. D. Young. 1977. The David Kopay Story. New York: Arbor House.

Lehne, G. H. 1989. "Homophobia Among Men: Supporting and Defining the Male Role." In *Men's Lives*, M. S. Kimmell and M. A. Messner, ed., pp. 416-29. New York: MacMillan.

Lenskyj, H. 1986. *Out of Bounds: Women, Sport and Sexuality*. Toronto: The Women's Press.

Pronger, B. 1990. *The Arena of Masculinity: Sports, Homosexuality, and the Meaning of Sex*. New York: St. Martin's Press.

Gay Athletes and the Gay Games: An Interview with Tom Waddell

MIKE MESSNER

In 1982, a history-making event took place in San Francisco. Thirteen hundred athletes from twelve different nations gathered for the first-ever Gay Games. The story of the Games is the story of the growth of a community. It is also the story of the evolution of a gay man, Tom Waddell, who for years kept his sexual orientation secret while competing as a world-class decathlete in the highly homophobic world of organized sports. Waddell was a leader in the gay community and the founder of the Gay Games. Although he was a physician, he was spending most of his time preparing for the 1986 Games and working for the American Civil Liberties Union when I interviewed him in 1984. I visited Tom in his San Francisco office, where I had the pleasure of talking with him about his life as a gay athlete and how the Gay Games fit into his vision of the future.

Tom: When I was a kid, I was tall for my age, and I was very thin but very strong. And I was usually faster than most other people. But I discovered rather early that I liked gymnastics and I liked dance. I was very interested in being a ballet dancer, and I studied with my mother until I was about seventeen and she said, "I can't teach you any more—you need to go to New York now." I had lived in New Jersey, so I started studying in New York. And something became obvious to me right away—that male ballet dancers were effeminate, that they were what most people would describe as faggots. And I thought I just couldn't handle that. It suddenly occurred to me that this was real dangerous territory for me—I'm from a small town and I was totally closeted and very concerned about being male . . . . This was in the fifties, a terrible time to live, and everything was stacked against me. Anyway, I realized that I had to do something to protect my image of myself as a male—because at that time homosexuals were thought of primarily as men who really would prefer to be women. And so I threw myself into athletics—I played football, gymnastics, track and field. I went to college on a gymnastics scholarship, was a nine-letter man through college, and I won all sorts of athletic awards and what-have-you. And I tried out for the Olympic team in 1960 and finished sixth in the tryouts. . . . I was a *jock*—that's how I was viewed, and I was comfortable with that, except that I suddenly realized in my junior year, I don't want to be a jock all my life—*just* a jock. So then I went to medical school.

During medical school he "literally forgot about athletics." He completed his internship, did a stint in the Army, and then at age thirty-four he finished an impressive sixth in the decathlon at the stormy 1968 Olympics in Mexico City. At this time—

Tom: I felt that I hadn't really achieved my peak yet. I was still concerned about, somewhere in my mind, wanting to protect a male image—I mean I was very much aware of that.

Mike: When you talk about protecting a male image, are you talking about the self that you're presenting to the world, or are you talking about how you feel about yourself?

Tom: How people viewed me. I was very comfortable with how I felt about myself. I had met a man a few years earlier who taught me internally to be at peace with myself, that being homosexual is okay.

Mike: I'm interested in that transition you went through from dance to sports.

Tom: I think ballet dancers are the greatest athletes in the world—far and away—it takes such coordination, strength, endurance. . . . In the past twenty years, it's changed here—boys get into it fairly young and it's okay to be a dancer now. You don't have to be queer to be a dancer. I just liked dancing. I mean, I liked moving, I liked the motion. I liked the finiteness of the motions in ballet—that here was a historical significance to all the moves, and they were labeled, and different people could execute them in different ways. To me, track and field is that same kind of beauty. When I watch runners, I just see motion in its most beautiful form—someone running for speed. Or a pole-vaulter or a high jumper—here's someone propelling their body through the air to achieve a particular thing. Now whether it's a jeté or a world record in the high jump doesn't make any difference—it's that particular kind of motion, it's very beautiful to me.

Mike: Did you feel sad when you left ballet?

Tom: No. I felt sad much later when I felt, hey, I could have been a dancer—I could have handled all this. See, I grew up thinking that I was the only gay person in the world.

During his athletic career, he struggled with his identity as a closeted gay man in the world of organized sports, where homophobia is "rampant."

Tom: You see, I think a lot of athletes go into athletics for the same reason that I did. They need to prove their maleness. I did, I readily admit it. I wanted to be viewed as male, otherwise I would be a dancer today. I wanted the male, macho image of an athlete. So I was protected with a very hard shell. And I was *clearly* aware of what I was doing.

Mike: When people associated gayness with femininity, it seems like that really bothered you.

Tom: Yeah, it did. I didn't feel that their reference points, as far as femininity, applied to me.

Mike: Did you feel an attachment to more traditional male traits?

Tom: Yeah, I mean athletically I was just as aggressive and hostile on the football field as anybody else. I loved knocking people down—I mean, I *liked* running over people—the whole thing was *fun.* And, uh, I've examined that often. I've examined my whole competitiveness in the Olympics, for example. . . . I often felt compelled to go along with a lot of locker room garbage because I wanted that image—and I know a lot of others who did, too. And I think many athletes are attracted to athletics because they're fighting their feminine qualities—they don't want to be seen that way. I know a lot of football players who very quietly and secretly like to paint, or play piano. And they do it quietly because this to them is threatening if it's known by others.

Toward the end of his athletic career, living in the closet became "so uncomfortable, so hot," that he finally decided to come out.

Tom: I had wanted to come out earlier and my friends always discouraged me—you know, "That'll create problems for you." Well, I already *had* problems, and the problems had to do with hiding. I was willing to face the new problems. To me, they were preferable to the ones I was having. . . . So I did come out publicly, in 1976, in *People Magazine.* I didn't do it in any small way! And you know, it's interesting, of the hundreds of people that I wrote to before I came out, only two people stopped talking to me. Both of them were world-class athletes—both of whom I think have real problems with their own sexual identities... It

In the early 1970s, Waddell kept his sexual identity "protected with a very hard shell" in his role as a world-class athlete. But eventually, living in the closet became so "uncomfortable, so hot," he decided to come out.

just scared the hell out of them when I came out—they didn't want to be guilty by association, so they just cut me off completely.

Tom Waddell became very involved with community activities in the San Francisco Bay Area. He rekindled his interest in the arts and in dance. He also remained very active in athletics. In 1982 Tom Waddell's brainchild, the Gay Games, took place for the first time in San Francisco. Waddell's vision was a radical break from the traditional notion of the role of sports in society, and the Gay Games reflected his values and his vision of building an "exemplary community" based upon equality and universal participation. Despite, or perhaps because of, this vision, the United States Olympic Committee (USOC) went to court to see that the word olympics was not used by gays to denote their Games. As Waddell explained,

Tom: See, there's a Police Olympics occurring now. Yeah, and they use the same symbol, the flame, and the five rings—the bottom two are handcuffs, but it's still the five rings.

Mike: That's a nice touch.

Tom: Yeah, and *they've* never been touched by the U.S. Olympic Committee, 'cause that's "Mom and apple pie." But we're queer. The whole thing is that they have a real problem with homosexuality—and they don't want to see the words "gay" and "olympics" in any combination. "Police," okay. "Special," okay. "Senior," okay. "Xerox," okay. "Armenian," okay. I mean, these are all Olympics that exist. "Crab cooking," okay, but not "Gay." Why don't they attack the Armenians, for instance? Because *they* don't do nasty things in bed. The whole thing's just stupid, you know. Here the courts are just knuckling under because of the power of the USOC. I mean, we're fighting corporate America here—a lot of special-interest groups are involved in this. I'm sure the Coca-Cola company says to the USOC.: "Hey! We're sponsoring the Olympics! We don't want 'Gay' out there!"

Mike: In terms of your personal involvement, what do the Games mean to you?

Tom: To me, it's one of those steps in a thousand-mile journey to try and raise consciousness and enlighten people—not just people outside the gay community, but within the gay community as well. When they come to the ghetto, they bring all the prejudices that they learned from the dominant society. We have 'em all there: we're just as racist, and ageist, sexist, nationalistic, and chauvinistic as anybody else. So it seems to me if a subculture's gonna form, that somehow we've gotta make ourselves exemplary. And how do we do that? Let's use that same process of self-liberation that we learned through coming out to get at other issues. Let's get at the sexism issue. Let's get at the ageism issue. Let's make ourselves an exemplary community.

So that's my vision of what the Games are about—it's just a step—it's a way of bringing a lot of people together and specifically addressing all those issues with these games. We have age-group competition, so all ages are involved. We have parity—if there's a men's sport, there's a women's sport to complement it. And we go out and recruit in Third World and minority areas. All of these people are gonna get together for a week, they're gonna march in together, march out together, they're gonna hold hands, and they'll say "Jesus Christ! This is wonderful!" There's this discovery: "I had no idea women were such fun!" and "God! Blacks are okay. . . . I didn't do anything to offend him, and we became friends!" and "God, that guy over there's in his sixties, and I had no idea they were so sexually active!" [He laughs.] Maybe it's simplistic to some people, but you know, why does it have to be complicated? Put people in a position where they can experience this process of discovery, and here it is!

Every time I speak, people go, "Oh, God, here he goes with his visions again!" Well, I realize that I might die before I see any of these things really grab—and most likely that'll be the case—but I just hope that this is something that'll take hold and a lot of people will get the idea. Everybody's welcome! Let's get together and have a festival—a People's Games.

AIDS, Homophobia, and Sports

MIKE MESSNER

Since Magic Johnson's highly publicized announcement in 1991 that he was retiring from professional basketball because he had been diagnosed as HIV-positive, and since Arthur Ashe, a once great tennis player, announced in 1992 that he had AIDS, and died of the disease in 1993, there has been increased public discussion of AIDS as a potentially major health crisis among athletes. But so far the public spotlight has fallen mostly on Johnson and Ashe, two famous athletes. Little notice has been given the approximately forty male figure skaters and figure-skating coaches in North America who have died of AIDS in recent years. With very few exceptions, the sports world has been slow to come to grips with the issue of AIDS. This is probably not because coaches, trainers, and team doctors are unconcerned about preventing diseases of the body. It's just that for the sports establishment to realistically deal with AIDS would require its confronting a major disease of the soul that has been a fixture in organized sports for decades: homophobia.

The extent of homophobia in the sports world is staggering: manifestations range from eight-year old boys who put each other down with taunts of "queer," "faggot," or "sissy" to high-school locker-room boasting (and, often, lying) about sexual conquests of females, and to college athletes bonding together with a little Saturday night "queer-bashing." To be suspected of being gay, and to be unable to prove one's heterosexual status in the sports world, is clearly not acceptable—indeed, it can be downright dangerous. For instance, in 1987, Tom Cousineau, a pro-football player, held a press conference to dispel the "insidious" rumor that he was gay. His previous employer, the Cleveland Browns, had actually assigned their security people to investigate Cousineau's "alleged sexual activities." "We found absolutely nothing," they reported, yet the "ugly rumor" persisted and followed Cousineau to his new job with the San Francisco 49ers. In a prepared statement, Cousineau went beyond simply declaring that he was a heterosexual: "Homosexuality has no place in my life. Never has and never will. . . . Given the times, calling a man gay is the fastest way to tearing him down. I don't want to be associated with that group of people. Personally, that thought repulses me." (Note: Cousineau quote from San Francisco Chronicle—date unknown.)

Given the extent of homophobia among athletes, coaches, fans, and the sports media, it is understandable that an athlete (whether he is in fact gay or not) would want to present an unambiguously heterosexual identity to the public. But Brian Pronger points out, in *The Arena of Masculinity* (1990), that many men playing organized sports at all levels are in fact closeted gays. David Kopay, a former pro-football player, suggested the same thing in his autobiography (*The David Kopay Story*, 1977) and Tom Waddell, a former Olympic athlete, told me, "I know a lot of world-class and professional athletes are gay." But those very few high-level male athletes who do choose to come out (as Kopay and Waddell did) find it prudent to do so only *after* retiring from their athletic careers. Coming out sooner would be too risky.

Magic Johnson has repeatedly had to deal with questions about his sexual orientation; rumors that he was gay or bisexual had circulated for years before the announcement of his HIV-positive status. To his credit, Johnson did not utter such anti-gay sentiments as had Cousineau, but he did go out of his way to emphasize that he had contracted the virus through *heterosexual* promiscuity: he claimed that he had had sexual relations with approximately twenty-five hundred women. Though this may seem a shockingly high figure, Johnson's tally pales in comparison with Wilt Chamberlain's claim to have had sex with twenty thousand women. Arthur Ashe, in his posthumously published book *Days of Grace* (1993), wrote that he felt a sense of "racial embarrassment" at Johnson's and Chamberlain's claims, because they reinforced the cultural stereotype of black males as amoral, oversexed beasts. One wonders if racial stereotypes contribute to the media's interest in these cases of promiscuous black athletes. The vilification of Wade Boggs, a white baseball star, for sexual promiscuity didn't create nearly the media frenzy that Johnson's and Chamberlain's stories did. And Arthur Ashe emphasized that his own sport of tennis, "for all its white, upper-class associations, is also a haven of promiscuity and easy sex."

The emergent discourse about heterosexual promiscuity among famous male athletes reveals many of the assumptions about male sexuality that lie at the heart of the AIDS problem. For instance, shortly after Magic Johnson announced his HIV-positive status, he was asked how he could possibly have sex with so many different women. He replied (as did many other professional athletes in the ensuing days and weeks) that scores of beautiful women hang around famous male jocks. Johnson implied that with that much "temptation," men such as himself are "weak," and he said that he felt a need to "accommodate" as many of these women as possible. Neo-Victorian assumptions about male sexuality underlie these claims of male weakness in the face of irresistible female sexual temptation. Men, in this view, have a nearly uncontrollable sexual drive. It is thus women's duty to impose moral restraint. If the women won't restrain themselves—or worse, *if the women actively come on to men*—then men have little choice but to "accommodate" these voracious women. Boys will be boys. They can't help it. It's their dicks talking. And so on.

Johnson's announcement that he is HIV-positive was not followed by any appreciable criticism of him as a person, nor, apparently, did it lessen his commercial value. He appears, in fact, to be more popular than ever. Undoubtedly, this is partly due to the love and respect that many people already had for Johnson. But the mostly positive public response to Magic Johnson's announcement is probably also partly due to his skillful presentation of his acquisition of the HIV virus as an unfortunate result of too much heterosexual manliness. By telling about his heterosexual exploits, Johnson managed to distance himself from the stigma attached to the many gay men and intravenous drug users who have also contracted the AIDS virus.

In fact, as pointed out by Martina Navratilova, a great tennis player, by positioning himself as an unambiguously heterosexual male, Magic Johnson has benefited from a double standard that is at the heart of the gender and sexual politics of American sports. While taking care not to attack Johnson personally, but instead highlighting the biases inherent in the sports world, Navratilova said,

> If I had the AIDS virus, would people be understanding? No, because they'd say I'm gay. . . . That's why they're accepting it with him, because he supposedly got it through heterosexual contact. There have been other athletes who died from AIDS, and they were pushed aside because they either got it from drugs or they were gay. If it had happened to a heterosexual woman who had been with one hundred or two hundred men, they'd call her a whore and a slut, and the corporations would drop her like a lead balloon. (Los Angeles Times, November 21, 1991)

Indeed, there is little doubt that Martina Navratilova and Billie Jean King, arguably the most important female tennis players in the post-World War II era, have lost potential income (especially money they might have earned for corporate endorsements) because of their public acknowledgments that they are, respectively, lesbian and bisexual.

But the final point that Navratilova made is very important too. Even heterosexual female athletes would likely be stigmatized and denied opportunities for corporate endorsements if it came to light that they had been sexually promiscuous. Male athletes, in contrast, are expected to be heterosexually promiscuous.

OUT OF THE CLOSETS

The AIDS epidemic has clearly upped the ante for a secretly gay male athlete who might be considering the already very risky move of "coming out of the closet." As a result, the locker room, where compulsory heterosexuality is a key component of an obsessively narrow definition of masculinity, is likely to remain a tightly sealed closet in the foreseeable future. This is why I believe Tom Waddell was such an important person in recent sports history, and why institutions like the Gay Games have such continued importance. When I met Tom Waddell in 1984, I was immediately convinced that he was one of the most remarkable men I had ever met. His list of accomplishments was impressive enough: a sixth place finish in the decathlon in the 1968 Olympics, a successful career as a physician, and the founding of the Gay Games. But it was not his accomplishments so much as his magnetic optimism that most deeply impressed me. Here was a strong and gentle man who contradicted two popularly held stereotypes: that of the athlete as an unreflective hypermasculine brute; and that of the gay man as limp-wristed and weak. He was a man who (in the Reagan era, no less!) retained his belief that racism, sexism, homophobia, and violence could be overcome. And he was *doing* something about it.

In the summer of 1986, several weeks before Gay Games II, Tom Waddell was diagnosed as having AIDS. He recovered his health long enough to preside over the Games and, incidentally, to win the Gold Medal in the javelin throw. What most impressed me when I saw a TV interview with Waddell several months after the Games was that he had apparently not lost his optimism. He bravely faced death—as many of his friends had already done—and continued to project the same hope that had served as the basis of his life: hope that together, people can build a world free from prejudices born of ignorance, and crippling

Arthur Ashe, who died of AIDS related illnesses in 1993, was critical both of the boastful sexual promiscuity of some male athletes and of the sports media's tendency to project negative sexual stereotypes on to black male athletes.

inequalities. He even saw a silver lining to the AIDS epidemic: "If gays want to be proud about something, they should be very proud about their response to the AIDS crisis."

Tom Waddell died on July 11, 1987, and hundreds of people gathered in the San Francisco City Hall rotunda to honor his memory. The city's health commissioner, James M. Foster, said that Waddell was "more than a doctor. Tom was also a healer. He was motivated by healing not only the diseases of the body, but diseases of the soul as well." Though he is gone, Tom Waddell's ideals and hopes live on with the people who were touched by him, and in the institution of the Gay Games. The purpose of the Games is "to educate people through sport in a spirit of understanding." The Games also offer an alternative structure in which gay men, lesbians, bisexuals, and even heterosexuals can forge their own definitions of athleticism, unfettered by the often oppressive stereotypes of the dominant sports world. As Tom Waddell pointed out, in the Gay Games participants learn that

> You don't win by beating someone else. We defined winning as doing your very best. That way, everyone is a winner. . . . I don't know that it's possible that this kind of attitude will prevail. It's revolutionary. And it's certainly not what the NFL owners or the United States Olympic Committee wants to hear, where winning is essential. So this is not going to be a popular attitude unless we *make* it a popular attitude.

Gay Games III were successfully held in Vancouver in 1990, and the organizers expect fifteen thousand athletes from over fifty countries to attend Gay Games IV in New York City in 1994. In a development that a few years ago even Tom Waddell might have thought impossible, the executive committee of the Federation of Gay Games recently initiated a "very positive and productive" dialogue about AIDS in sports with a former nemesis, the U.S. Olympic Committee. Maybe Tom Waddell's simple idea *is* catching on. As Waddell's former Olympics teammate Bill Toomey said of Waddell through his own tears, "He's a very valuable person to this planet, and I'll always think that." I couldn't agree more.

REFERENCES

Ashe, Arthur. 1993. *Days of Grace*. New York: Alfred A. Knopf.

Kopay, D., and P. D. Young. 1977. *The David Kopay Story*. New York: Arbor House.

Pronger, B. 1990. *The Arena of Masculinity: Sports, Homosexuality, and the Meaning of Sex*. New York: St. Martin's Press.

Part V
MARGINAL MEN

We know that sports are one key way in which boys and men in modern societies express their masculinity. But when we look at which boys and men play and excel in sports, we see that expressions of athletic masculinity are far more common among certain groups. As Bob Connell, an Australian sociologist, has suggested, it makes sense to speak not of a singular masculinity, but rather of an array of coexisting "masculinities." A "marginalized masculinity" may be constructed by men who, because of low social status, low levels of education, racism, homophobia, or incarceration, lack access to legitimate means of expressing the dominant white, middle-class, heterosexual form of masculinity. For many young, marginalized men, sports participation and athletic careers turn out to be one of the few legitimate means of establishing a respected masculinity. Indeed, a highly disproportionate number of top-level football, basketball, and track-and-field athletes are African Americans, while United States-born Latinos and Latin Americans have a disproportionate presence in professional baseball. Boxing, too, is dominated by African Americans and Latinos. In all these sports, the whites who rise to the top tend to come from poor and blue-collar families. It is only the "country-club sports," such as tennis, golf, and swimming, that are dominated by middle- and upper-class whites.

Sports participation and athletic careers, then, tend to take on different meanings for boys and young men from different racial, ethnic, and class backgrounds. But rather than acknowledging the different socio-economic and cultural backgrounds that lead some boys to emphasize sports, our schools too often assume a racist mind-body split when it comes to boys and sports. Whites from middle-class families are channeled into college-prep classes. If they play sports, they are often placed in high-status, decision-making positions such as quarterback. Meanwhile, young black males are often seen as "natural athletes" who are believed to have little or no aptitude in academics, and no leadership qualities on the playing fields. This assumption can become a self-fulfilling prophecy, with organized sports serving to perpetuate race and class inequalities.

The sports media, too, have often reinforced widely held stereotypes about "natural" differences between African Americans and whites. But racial stereotypes in sports media are being challenged and discarded. For instance, in 1989 a *Boston Globe* reporter, Derrick Jackson, published a study that showed how football commentators tended to attribute the successes of black football players to their "natural abilities," while attributing the successes of white players to "brains" and "hard work." A study of televised sports conducted a year later revealed almost none of this kind of racial stereotyping by sports commentators. Why? Shortly after Jackson's research was published, Arthur Ashe, a former tennis player, said "word came down from the top"—from executives at the TV network for which he was doing sports commentary—that "we should stop attributing black athletes' successes to 'brawn' and white athletes' successes to 'brains and hard work.' "

Subtle racism still persists in sports commentary and reporting. But we are encouraged by the fact that the sports media has responded to criticism based on solid research. Some schools are turning away from racism in sports, too, by taking more responsibility for the education and futures of black male student athletes. As the following articles suggest, these changes are only beginnings. But these changes offer hope that rather than continuing to reinforce racial stereotypes and social inequalities, sports might bring together the privileged with the socially marginalized boys and men to discover their common humanity.

Sports and the Politics of Inequality

MIKE MESSNER

Our town had two high schools. Ours was mostly the poor and blue-collar workers and the rich kids all went to Northside. They always beat us in sports, but my senior year we had a good basketball team, and we all really hoped we could beat Northside. Well, by the middle of the first half our team was just totally *dominating* them—it was amazing—and the crowd on our side did this cheer, "IN YOUR *FACE*, NORTHSIDE!" After a couple of minutes, the Northside crowd yelled back, "THAT'S ALL RIGHT, THAT'S OK, YOU'LL BE WORKING FOR *US* SOMEDAY!"

This story, told by a young man about his high-school experience in a small Midwestern town, illuminates some of the complex and contradictory aspects of sports in a society stratified along ethnic and class lines. Since a typical sporting contest seems to exist outside the realm of everyday social experience, it theoretically should be able to bring together people of diverse cultural and economic backgrounds. Every person is supposed to have the same opportunity to excel, is to be judged by the same standards, and must conform to the same set of rules under the watchful eyes of a neutral authority (the referee) and the community. The game thus reinforces myths of fairness, equal opportunity, meritocracy, and democracy.

But simmering just below the surface of this seemingly egalitarian contest are the hatreds, prejudices, and antagonisms that result from social inequality. When participation in sports is open to all in a stratified society, the sporting arena often becomes a contested terrain where intergroup antagonisms are played out. For the blue-collar kids (and for their fans and families in the stands), the game becomes a vehicle for proving that "we're just as good as they are—maybe we're even better." For a fleeting moment, the working class can achieve victory and shove it in the faces of their superiors. But this victory is immediately shoved back into their faces as meaningless in terms of life *outside* the sporting arena: inequality still exists after the final buzzer sounds, and the privileged classes have the luxury of pooh-poohing the importance of a mere game compared with real life, in which "you'll be working for *us* someday."

From the point of view of many who are concerned with the problems of the poor, the oppressed in this society, the experience of athletes often seems meaningless. Some regard sports as an "opiate" that keeps vital energies diverted from important political and economic tasks. But another viewpoint is not so immediately obvious: what goes on in the sporting arena is meaningful in understanding the making and remaking of social reality. When poor people, working-class people, and black or brown people compete with the dominant classes and achieve some success in sports, this does not automatically eliminate poverty and inequality, but it does change the context in which class and race relations take place.

When boys and men from different racial and socioeconomic backgrounds meet on the athletic fields, the contest sometimes takes on a greater meaning than simply a "game."

REINFORCING RACISM

Organized sports were originally set up in Britain and in the United States by white upper-class males to measure themselves against each other and to "build character" in preparation for roles as leaders in business and industry. As long as this apartheid-like system existed, the athletic accomplishments of white males from the upper classes could be used as an ideological justification for existing social inequalities. Blacks, women, and other oppressed groups, it was argued, could not compete with white males in sports or in the economy because they would surely lose, given their "obvious" inherent inferiority.

But as some color bars began to fall in professional and amateur sports—Satchel Paige striking out top white professional baseball players in an exhibition, Jesse Owens capturing the Olympic Gold in Munich in 1936, Jackie Robinson excelling in the previously all-white professional baseball leagues—the old myth of white superiority was challenged. Today, athletes still symbolically embody the hopes and dreams—and the prejudices—of different communities. For example, many whites hoped that Gerry Cooney would be the "Great White Hope" who finally won the heavyweight boxing championship. And a black friend told me that Larry Bird, the Boston Celtics' star, is the second most hated man in the black community (after Ronald Reagan) for daring to be among the best in a "black sport."

Behind the legendary giants of professional sports are millions of athletes who compete in high schools, in recreation leagues, and on playgrounds. Harry Edwards, a sociologist, argues that hundreds of thousands of black youth are "channeled" into sports by role models in the media, by encouragement from peers and family, and by the denial of access to white-dominated schools and professions. Far from indicating progress for blacks, the predominance of blacks in many sports indicates the persistence of racism in society. And, as Edwards and others have pointed out, the amount of harm that results can be staggering, since an incredibly small number of people ever actually make a living through sports. According to Edwards (1984)

> Despite the fact then that American basketball, boxing, football, and baseball competitions have come more and more to look like Ghana playing Nigeria, sport nonetheless looms like a fog-shrouded minefield for the overwhelming majority of black athletes. It has been a treadmill to oblivion rather than the escalator to wealth and glory it was believed to be. There is today disturbingly consistent evidence that the black athlete who blindly sets out to fill the shoes of Dr. J., Reggie J., Magic J., Kareem Abdul-J., or O. J. is destined to end up with "No J."—no job whatsoever that he is qualified to do in our modern, technologically sophisticated society. At the end of his career, he is not running through airports like O. J. He is much more likely to be sweeping up airports—if he has the good fortune to land even that job.

Are organized sports simply a social mechanism through which social inequalities are perpetuated and justified? Are there perhaps moments in sports—especially for the majority of participants who never come close to "making it big"—that might lead to the opposite tendencies? Specifically, does the day-to-day interaction of males "playing together" on the nation's playgrounds lead to a breakdown of racism and to a discovery of our common humanity with which we can challenge the inequities of the larger society?

IN YOUR FACE!

I drove the lane and put up what I thought was a pretty good-looking jump-hook in heavy traffic when, seemingly from nowhere, a large black hand swatted the ball away. "Try to come in here again with that weak shit and I'll kick your white ass!" This was my introduction to Ron, who appeared to me the epitome of the black playground player: with his gangly six-foot-four-inch frame, his shaved head, his quickness and style, his aggressive intensity, and his frequent verbal intimidation, he would usually dominate play at this mostly white playground that I came to frequent.

After playing in pickup games with Ron for three years (yet rarely speaking with him), I decided he would be an interesting person to interview for my research on athletes. He quickly agreed ("You gonna make me *famous*?"). Although my goal was to learn about "the Black Athlete," my interview with this good-humored and thoughtful thirty-year-old "professional gym-rat" ultimately taught me more about my own deeply ingrained attitudes and assumptions concerning black males. I admitted to Ron that his verbal and physical aggressiveness had certainly intimidated me. When playing against him I found myself playing much more passively, simply out of fear that if I "took the ball to the hoop," he would embarrass me—or even hurt me. Ron laughed and told me that he had consciously constructed much of his style to intimidate "white boys" like me and get the edge over them.

> I'm tall, I'm thin, I'm a black person with a shaved head, and I'm fearful. You have to intimidate mentally, because that's the advantage you have. But you're not really out to hurt that individual—it's competitiveness—the whole realization is that you've *gotta* talk shit in this game, you *have* to say, you know, "If you come close to me, I'm gonna *hurt* you!"

I asked Ron if he had ever had to back up that bluster with his fists, and his answer was a real revelation to me: "No, never. Are you kidding? Never." He laughed. "I would run. I would *run*. I'd be scared to fight." Now, I've played basketball since I was old enough to count to two, and it had never occurred to me that the black players might be a bit scared, too. It's fascinating to me to realize that I have always been a little more tentative—even passive—when playing against black guys, and that underlying this tentativeness has been my fear of what I assumed to be a potential for violence simmering just below the surface of that black skin. Where did this assumption come from? Certainly not from personal experience—never had a black player physically attacked me in a game. But the fear has been there, nonetheless. And, semiconsciously, I have always felt that winning a particular game just wasn't so important if it meant that I had to get my face smashed in for it. If it's so important to him that he has to threaten me, then by God he can *have* the damned game! (Am I mistaken, or is there a faint echo of "You'll be working for *us* someday," here?)

Interestingly, even though my talk with Ron disturbed me in that it made me aware of how deeply ingrained my own racist attitudes are, it also raised my hopes that sports can be an activity in which racism is undermined. Ron spent a good deal of time talking to me about how he met his best friend—a white man—on a basketball court. When they play on the same team together, he told me, "We know each other's moves so well it's like magic sometimes."

SPORTS AND THE POLITICS OF INEQUALITY

If this discussion of sports and inequality seems to make contradictory points, it is because sports play a contradictory role in the larger politics of inequality. Ideologically, sports strengthen and legitimate class and ethnic inequalities while simultaneously providing space where prejudices can be challenged and debunked. For participants, sports offer a place where class and ethnic antagonisms can be destructively played out *and* where participants can experience transcendent moments of play that are relatively free from the larger social inequities. In sports, it is possible to discover ourselves and each other as human beings. What all this means is that the role sports will play in the politics of inequality will be determined by "how we play the game," both individually and collectively.

REFERENCES

Edwards, Harry. 1984. "The Collegiate Athletic Arms Race." *Journal of Sport and Social Issues* 8 (1) pp. 4-22.

White Men Misbehaving: Feminism, Afrocentrism, and the Promise of a Critical Standpoint

MIKE MESSNER

A year or so ago I was called on the phone by a representative of the National Organization for Women (NOW) Legal Defense and Education Fund, who was searching for a male academic who would publicly take a stand against the controversial movement in Detroit to establish all-male public schools in predominantly African-American districts. "Well," I waffled, "I'm not for it, but I do understand how the deteriorating conditions in urban communities and schools, and the especially devastating impact on young African American males, have led

ote: This essay is adapted from a keynote address at the North American Society for the Sociology of ual Meetings in Toledo, Ohio, on November 6, nks to Pierrette Hondagneu-Sotelo for helpful com- an earlier draft.

many African Americans to desperately search for solutions."

"Yes," the NOW representative replied, "We know that, too, but our position is that there is no evidence that separating boys from girls is going to solve these problems. In fact, we are worried that this approach ignores the problems faced by African American girls, and will justify tipping more educational resources away from them. Would you be willing to testify on behalf of our position?"

"Well," I sidestepped and backpedalled, "I really think it's more appropriate that you find African American scholars to talk about this."

In the end, I passed up the opportunity to take a public stand on this issue. My gut-level reason was that I felt that it was inappropriate for me, a white male academic, to take a public stand against a grassroots initiative in an African American community. But I also felt that in taking no public stand on this issue, I had failed in my commitment to support women's quest for equality. After having spent much of my time in the past few years researching, writing, and teaching about the ways that race, class, gender, and sexual systems of oppression often intersect, my theories, it seemed, were revealed as useless ivory-tower exercises. I felt, in short, like a bit of a chump.

After pondering this incident for some time, I'm a bit less hard on myself. I am convinced, though, that the controversy raised some fundamental issues that should be explored and publicly discussed. The primary question that I will focus on here is how we can conceptualize the relationships between racial and gender oppression. In particular, I will discuss how African American males stand in very contradictory manner at the nexus of intersecting systems of racial and gender oppression. But conceptualizing and theorizing is clearly not enough. Also at issue is how to connect theory and research to the real world. How, as Russell Jacoby (1987) asked, does one serve as a responsible "public intellectual?" I think the key question is not "Should my research be engaged with the real world?" but rather, "Whose interests should my research serve?" I could easily respond to this question by asserting that I aim for my work to serve "the oppressed," against the interests of the oppressors. But the answer is clearly not that simple. When progressive groups perceive their interests as conflicting—as happened in the Detroit case, in which an African American community attempting to take control of their schools came into conflict with feminists—our theories are revealed to be inadequate.

I believe it will prove fruitful to explore this intersection of race and gender by examining two ascendant schools of thought about African American males: Afrocentrism and Black Feminism.* The current dialogue between these two political discourses offers a new perspective on the study of sports and culture. This perspective may help us gain not only a clearer understanding of how race and gender interact in the lives of African American women and men, but also a critical perspective on hegemonic masculinity as a problem, rather than as a universal normative standard.

YOUNG BLACK MALES AND AFROCENTRISM

In the spring of 1992, I experienced the Los Angeles Rebellions as most everybody else did: I watched them on television, though for an L.A. resident like me, the smell of smoke and the constant sound of helicopters overhead added a troubling dimension of realism to the televised spectacle. One moment in the televised coverage stays with me more than any other. As I watched what appeared to be three young white men jumping up and down on a car and smashing it with crowbars, the news commentator's voice-over said, "Black youth are rampaging in the South-Central area." At that moment, I was reminded of an article I had recently read by Stuart Alan Clarke (1991), in which he asserts that American society is obsessed with images of "black men misbehaving." Indeed, I thought, even when our eyes clearly show us a scene of young *white* men "misbehaving," the media still tend to portray the black male as the villain.

*I take the term "black feminist thought" from Collins (1990), and acknowledge the limitations built into the concept. First, to speak of "black feminist thought" risks rendering other women of color—Asian, Native American, Chicana, and Latina—invisible. Second, the concept tends toward a racial essentialism. As Collins acknowledges, there really is no way to define who is and who is not "black," due to the fact that such racial categories are socially constructed. Nevertheless, it is useful and important to acknowledge a somewhat distinct standpoint emerging from women who identify themselves as African American.

Young black males are very aware of the general suspicion in which they're held. For instance, at the University of Southern California (USC) where I teach, a man who was described as a "tall, thin, thirtyish black male" attempted several rapes in a campus parking structure about two years ago. One of my black male students, who was twentyish, short, and stout, told me that he was put up against the wall and frisked by police on campus. He told me that "all of us black guys know to walk around campus with books and briefcases, dressed like students, or we'll be hassled by the police."

Woody Allen—whom I'm not so sure it is politically correct to quote these days—once said that "90 percent of success in life is just showing up." I suspect his statement applies more to white males from privileged backgrounds than to other people. There are abundant examples of not-so-talented white males who have managed to parlay their cultural capital into positions of power. In fact, in the case of Dan Quayle, Woody Allen may have understated his point. But for women, for poor people and blue-collar workers, for people of color, and for gays and lesbians, just showing up is not nearly enough—they must often fight for rights and for respect. Indeed, in my research with male former athletes, the black men often spoke of a desire for respect as a prime motivating force in their athletic strivings (Messner 1992). They knew from experience that black males, especially in public life, are far more likely to be *sus*pected than *res*pected. This shared experience of suspicion and lack of respect among African American males goes a long way toward explaining the organized—and I am sure in some ways ambivalent and agonized—support that Mike Tyson and Clarence Thomas received from some sectors of the African American community. The easy framing of Tyson as a sexual predator and an animal, in particular, played into all of the most destructive and racist stereotypes about black males in American society.

Young black males today are living with the legacy of twenty-plus years of deindustrialization, rising joblessness, and declining inner-city schools, and twelve years of Republican preaching to "just say no" to drugs and gangs, while the only things worth saying yes to crumble (Wilson 1987). As Elijah Anderson (1990) observes, the decline of solid blue-collar jobs for black males, along with the flight of much of the black middle class to the suburbs, has left young inner-city black males with few "old heads"—adult male community leaders, who have traditionally taught young males the values of hard work, family support, and community responsibility. Today, Anderson observes, the old heads have been replaced by the more respected "new heads"—young street toughs and drug dealers with wads of cash. For a very limited number of black male youths, one kind of old head remains: the inner-city coach. A moving photo essay in *Sports Illustrated* featured the Dorsey High School football team, in Southwest Los Angeles, and their coach, Paul Knox (Miller and Smith 1992). The text described Coach Knox and his assistants as "strong black men who serve not only as coaches, but as role models. They talk to their players like brothers. They listen to them like fathers. They try like hell to keep their players safe." From this piece, one gets the impression of life on the football team at Dorsey as a bit of an oasis within a war zone. As gunshots sound outside the stadium, teammates who belong to different gangs embrace and support each other.

Reading this article makes clear why athletic careers still appear to many young black males as the way "up and out" of the ghetto. Adult leaders might preach to these youths to emphasize "books first," but the

Young black males are often surrounded by an aura of constant suspicion. It is through athletic accomplishments that many of them hope to achieve the respect of others.

realities they experience every day tend to point them in different directions. For the athletically inclined, sports is one of these directions. No matter how much parents, teachers, and community leaders stress "books first," the college statistics for black male nonathletes are not encouraging. In the 1990 to 1991 academic year, only 6 percent of all students in Division I schools were African American,while 22.3 percent of all scholarship athletes, 42.7 percent of scholarship football players, and 59.9 percent of scholarship men's basketball players were black. At my university, where only 4.7 percent of all students are black, 31.8 percent of those on athletic scholarships are black, while 44.7 percent and 84.6 percent, respectively, of scholarship football players and men's basketball players are black (Lederman 1992).

Educators and sociologists can debate the question of whether encouraging young black males to pursue athletic careers is helpful or not. But the reality is that, when young boys from the neighborhood surrounding USC walk through campus, they see what must appear to be an ocean of mostly white faces and blonde hair. When they look out on the athletic training fields or in the gym, or watch a game on television, they see a very high proportion of blacks. I suspect that the reality they see with their own eyes speaks more loudly than any words.

African American males' shared knowledge of their increasingly limited educational and economic opportunities, and their day-to-day experience of Americans' obsession with "black men misbehaving," go a long way toward explaining the forms that progressive movements in African American communities are taking today. The current Afrocentric movement is surely not in the tradition of Martin Luther King's call for racial integration. Instead, it echoes Malcolm X's call for community autonomy. And, like the Muslim and Black Power movements of the 1960s, Afrocentrism today asserts a militant "black manhood."

Black manhood was depicted in the recent film "Boyz 'n the 'Hood." The film suggests that the young males in the 'hood are faced with two major options: the first is to follow the lead of the young hoodlum "new heads," and likely end up cycling in and out of prison and eventually getting killed at a young age. A second possibility is suggested in the case of a talented young football player who is being recruited by USC. This option, too, is revealed as a possible dead end, as the youth's talents and dreams cannot safeguard him from the violence in his community. Indeed, recently, one of USC's football players was struck during practice by a stray bullet from local gang violence. The incident demonstrates how thin the line between the street and the athletic field is for many of these young men. But "Boyz 'n the 'Hood" offers a ray of hope. Here, for one of the very few times in American cinema, a positive image of an African American father was presented. And this man's son, we see, eventually makes the right choices that allow him to escape the violent 'hood and attend college.The film's message was undoubtedly positive, but I was left with the same troubling question that the Detroit all-male schools issue raised: What about the women? To make its point that a strong father is the answer to the problem of black male youth, the film depicted the mothers of the youths as irresponsible crack addicts, unfair bitches, or upwardly mobile professionals who neglected their children for their careers.

BLACK FEMINISM AND THE GENDER POLITICS OF AFROCENTRISM

Twenty years ago, the masculinist gender politics of antiracist organizations were rarely questioned. The few black feminists, such as Michelle Wallace (1978), who challenged assumptions of male superiority by leaders such as Eldridge Cleaver or Stokely Carmichael were accused of undermining the cause of black liberation by dividing women from men. Today, with assertions of black manhood again taking center stage in Afrocentric discourse and political practice, black women are offering a broader, more assertive and sophisticated response. For example, at the American Sociological Association meetings in 1990 Elijah Anderson presented some of his ethnographic research (which he later published as *Streetwise*). Anderson told the following story, based on the narrative of a black man, of a late-night street interaction between three black males and a white woman:

> A white lady walkin' down the street with a pocketbook. She start walkin' fast. She get so paranoid she break into a little stride. Me and my friends comin' from a party about 12:00. She stops and goes up on the porch of a house, but you could tell she didn't live there. I stop and say, "Miss, you didn't have to do that. I thought you might think we're some wolf pack. I'm twenty-eight, he's twenty-six, he's twenty-nine. You ain't gotta run from us." She said, "Well, I'm sorry." I said, "You can come down. I know you don't live there. We just comin' from a party." We just walked down the street and she came back down, walked across the street where she really wanted to go. So she tried to act as though she lived there. And she didn't. After we said, "You ain't gotta run from us," she said, "No, I was really in a hurry." My boy said, "No you wasn't. You thought we was gon' snatch yo' pocketbook." We pulled money out. "See this, we work." I said, "We grown men, now. You gotta worry about them fifteen-, sixteen-, seventeen-year-old boys. That's what you worry about. But we're grown men." I told her all this. "They the ones ain't got no jobs; they're too young to really work. They're the ones you worry about, not us." She understood that. You could tell she was relieved and she gave a sigh. She came back down the steps, even went across the street. (Anderson 1990, 167-68).

The point of Anderson's story—that, in public places, black males are commonly unfairly suspected of being muggers or rapists—was well taken. But the woman in the story was a somewhat humorous prop for making this point about the indignities that black males face.

Anderson did not appear to have much empathy for her. As he finished telling the story, a white woman sitting in front of me whispered to the white woman next to her, "He acts like she had no reason to be frightened of a pack of men. Of *course* she was scared! Women are attacked and raped every day!" This woman empathized with the white woman in the story, but gave no indication that she understood Anderson's point about the impact of this omnipresent suspicion on the vast majority of black males who do not rape or rob. After the talk, during the discussion session, an African American woman stood up and bridged this chasm by eloquently empathizing with the legitimate fears of the woman *and* with the humiliation of the black males in the story. The woman and the men in this story, she asserted, were victimized in public space, but in different ways. The solution lies in their learning to empathize with each other, and then building from that common empathy a movement that fights against the oppressive system that dehumanizes them both.

This scene, it seemed to me, demonstrated both the limits of masculinist Afrocentrism and of white feminism, while demonstrating the role that black feminism can play in bridging these two movements. As Patricia Hill Collins (1990) has so eloquently put it, black women are often "outsiders within"—as women, they are outsiders within the Afrocentric movement; as blacks, they are outsiders within feminism. This social position "on the margins," to use bell hooks' (1984) terminology, gives black women a unique standpoint from which the complex mechanisms and interweavings of power and oppression can be more clearly deconstructed and, possibly, resisted. Black feminists acknowledge and decry black males' unique experiences of oppression. But black feminists do not accept the analysis by some men of color (e.g., Pena 1991 and Staples 1992) of rape, public displays of misogyny, and other forms of violence against women by men of color primarily as distorted or displaced responses to racism and to class constraints. Instead, black feminists view such violence not as a "superstructural" manifestation of class or racial politics, but as the product of a semiautonomous system of power relations between women and men.

In an essay on black masculinity, bell hooks (1992) charges that what she calls "conservative Afrocentric males" often draw on "phallocentric masculinity" as a resource to fight racial oppression. And, she observes, public figures such as Eddie Murphy and Spike Lee tend to exploit the commodification of phallocentric black masculinity. But, hooks argues, there *are* "progressive Afrocentric males," including many gay black men, who are "not sitting around worried about castration and emasculation," but are instead carrying on egalitarian relationships with women and with other men. The emergent dialogue between these progressive Afrocentric males and black feminists may inform critical studies of sports.

THE PROMISE OF A CRITICAL STANDPOINT IN SPORT STUDIES

Susan Birrell (1990) has suggested that we should build theory by listening to the "home truths" of the "critical autobiography" of women of color. Building on Birrell's suggestion, Yevonne Smith (1992, 228) has argued that more studies of women of color in sports would contribute to a more "inclusive womanist/feminist scholarship and race relations theory." I agree with Smith, and I am convinced that it would be most fruitful to listen to the public conversations taking place today between Afrocentric males and black feminist women. An example of such a conversation can be found in bell hooks' (1990) dialogue with Cornel West.

Even those of us who are not central players can learn from these conversations to ask new, critical questions. De-centered theoretically, we can begin to turn commonly asked questions back on themselves: "Why do black men so often misbehave?" becomes "Why are we so obsessed with this question, and what, in fact, about the everyday misbehaviors of *white* men, including middle- and upper-class white men?" Invisible in Elijah Anderson's street scene are the powerful white men, who, through their control of institutions, have removed jobs from the inner cities, cut school funds, allowed police protection for citizens to decline while allowing some police to engage in racist terror tactics, and refused to take the measures that might make public life safe for women, thus imposing on them a de facto curfew. Privileged males are invisible in this story because the race, class, and gendered power of these males is attached to their positions in institutions, not to their personal behaviors in the street. In fact, their everyday actions in political, corporate and educational institutions are considered normal male behavior. A key task for the present, it seems to me, is to raise critical questions about the normal operation of hegemonic masculinity in such a way that these actions are redefined as misbehaviors.

Black feminist thought offers a theoretical framework with which we might better understand the crucial issues of our day. For instance, with many colleges and universities today "downsizing," when women file Title IX suits intended to push educational institutions toward gender equity, one response by universities may be simply to cut sports, as Brooklyn College has done. This might cause males—especially those poor and black males who see athletic scholarships as their main hope for upward mobility—to oppose equal funding for women's sports.

Tension between defenders of men's sports—especially football—and advocates of women's sports is already evident. For instance, Donna Lopiano (1992), currently the head of the Women's Sports Foundation, has described a cartoon that she would like to see appear in *The Chronicle of Higher Education.* The cartoon, as Lopiano described it, would consist of a single frame in which a flock of geese, each with a potbelly and wearing a football helmet, would be flying in a V formation. The lead goose would be plummeting to the earth, a plume of smoke in its wake. Below, standing on the ground, would be two women, dressed in athletic uniforms and holding shotguns. One of them would be saying to the other, "Don't they know we're just shooting blanks?"

Lopiano's cartoon can represent a much more complex picture if we take into account more than simply the standpoint of the two women athletes. I picture the flock of geese (who represent men's football programs) as being 42.7 percent black, and flying over a campus community that is only 6 percent black. The lead goose, plummeting to the earth, is a young black man whose dream of an NFL contract has been dashed by a serious injury. One of the black geese is saying about the women who are shooting at them, "Don't they know that we have to dress up like this and learn to fly in formation in order to be allowed on this campus?" I envision yet a third party in this picture. Standing just at the margin, barely inside the frame, a black feminist speaks to both the geese and to the female athletes: "What are all of you fools *doing*? They've got you young men endangering your lives in a brutal game, so that all of these white people can watch you crash and burn and be carried off on stretchers. And they've got you women taking up arms and shooting at people, as though you are trying to mimic the worst things that men do. Isn't there something terribly wrong with the entire system that pits its victims against each other?"

In this imaginary picture, each of the three standpoints (of the female athletes, the male athletes, and the black feminist) offers a partial understanding of reality. But the black feminist standpoint, grounded as it is in the experience of double, and often triple, oppression and marginalization, is likely to offer the most radical view, in the sense of identifying the common causes of gender-, race-, and class-based oppressions. Black feminism invites us to shift our attention away from bickering between oppressed groups, and instead to focus our energies on developing a critical understanding of the power structure that frames and shapes this picture. From this critical standpoint, we may be able to respond to such issues as who should get athletic funding not by taking stands either with men against women or with women against men, but instead by building coalitions that confront the institutional conventions that so often pit us against one another.

REFERENCES

Anderson, E. 1990. *Streetwise: Race, Class, and Change in an Urban Community*. Chicago: University of Chicago Press.

Birrell, S. 1990. "Women of Color, Critical Autobiography, and Sport." In *Sport, Men and the Gender Order: Critical Feminist Perspectives*, ed. M. A. Messner and D. F. Sabo, 185-89. Champaign, IL: Human Kinetics.

Clark, S. A. 1991. "Fear of a Black Planet." *Socialist Review* 21(2): 37-59.

Collins, P. H. 1990. *Black Feminist Thought: Knowledge, Consciousness, and the Politics of Empowerment*. Boston: Unwin Hyman.

hooks, b. 1984. *Feminist Theory: From Margin to Center*. Boston: South End Press.

hooks, b. 1990. "Black Women and Men: Partnership in the 1990s." In *Yearning: Race, Gender, and Cultural Politics*, b. hooks, 203-14.Boston: South End Press.

hooks, b. 1992. "Reconstructing Black Masculinity." In *Black Looks: Race and Representation*, b. hooks, 87-114. Boston: South End Press.

Jacoby, R. 1987. *The Last Intellectuals: American Culture in the Age of Academe*. New York: Basic Books.
Lederman, D. 1992. "Blacks Make Up Larger Proportion of Scholarship Athletes, yet Their Overall Enrollment Lags at Division I Colleges." *Chronicle of Higher Education*, June 17.
Lopiano, D. 1992. "Quick Fix or Radical Surgery: Reform in College Athletics." Keynote address to the North American Society for the Sociology of Sport Meetings in Toledo, Ohio, on November 5.
Messner, M. A. 1992. *Power at Play: Sports and the Problem of Masculinity*. Boston: Beacon Press.
Miller, R. and S. Smith. 1992. "Up Against the Wall." *Sports Illustrated*, October 19, 44-53.
Pena, M. 1991. "Class, Gender and Machismo: The 'Treacherous Woman' Folklore of Mexican Male Workers." *Gender & Society* 5:30-46.
Smith, Y. R. 1992. "Women of Color in Society and Sport." *Quest* 44:228-50.
Staples, R. 1992. "Stereotypes of Black Masculinity: The Facts Behind the Myths." In *Men's Lives*, 2nd ed., ed. M. S. Kimmel and M. A. Messner, 432-38. New York: Macmillan.
Wallace, M. 1978. *Black Macho and the Myth of the Super-Woman*. New York: Warner Books.
Wilson, W. J. 1987. *The Truly Disadvantaged*. Chicago: University of Chicago Press.

Seen but Not Heard: Images of Black Men in Sports Media

DON SABO AND SUE CURRY JANSEN

Race and gender politics often converge in complex and confusing ways, especially in sports and the sports media. But whereas studies of racial stereotyping and scapegoating, and their effects on members of stigmatized social groups, have occupied a prominent place in social science research since the 1930s, the role of racial stereotyping and scapegoating in maintaining the prevailing (hegemonic) definitions of masculinity in the U.S. has attracted little attention. Here we explore the race-gender nexus in sports by examining some widely used conventions for "framing" images of black males in the sports media.

Black males are, of course, highly visible in sports and sports media, but there has been little research or analysis on how blacks are being portrayed in sports media. Ralph Linton described stereotypes as "pictures in our heads." Do the sports media reflect the "pictures" of

African American men that the white apologists for slavery and colonialism created centuries ago?

Many stereotypical traits commonly associated with black manhood—aggression, brute strength, and stupidity—are also associated with athleticism. The blending and blurring of images of black masculinity and athletic prowess in white consciousness became evident when Franz Fanon (1970) analyzed the free associations of white psychiatric patients. He found that the word Negro evoked characteristic responses, including "strong," "athletic," "potent," "savage," "animal."

SYSTEMATIC NEGATIVE REPRESENTATION

Overtly and covertly, sports media contribute to racial stereotyping, some research indicates. Rainville and McCormick (1977) analyzed transcripts of twelve televised National Football League (NFL) games to explore the extent of racial prejudice in professional football commentators' speech. They found that white players were praised more frequently than black players, and were more apt to be described as causal agents. Compared with blacks, whites also received more physical attributions (for example, "big John Smith") and positive cognitive attributions ("Bailey is trying to figure out what to do on this one"). Blacks, compared with whites, received significantly more references to past failures (for example, academic probation in college) and were more often described as externally moved objects rather than as causal agents. The researchers concluded that while the announcers' chatter helped build good reputations for white players, it cloaked black players with comparatively negative reputations.More recently, Derrick Jackson, of the *Boston Globe*, analyzed televised sports commentary on basketball and football in 1988 and 1989. Seven college basketball games were recorded, including three National Collegiate Athletic Association (NCAA) Final Four games as well as five NFL playoff games. Two university researchers were given transcripts of the commentaries; they had no knowledge of which comments were attributed to what players. They then classified all comments into four categories: "Brawn" (running, leaping, size, strength and quickness), "Brains" (intelligence, leadership, motivation), "Weakling" (lack of speed and size), and

"Dunce" (confused or out of emotional control). The results indicated marked stereotyping of blacks within the Brawn and Dunce categories:

- In football, 65 percent of all comments made about black athletes were in the Brawn category, as were only 17 percent of comments about white players.
- Black football players were 6 times more likely than whites to be classified as Dunces: 12 percent and 2 percent of comments, respectively, were in this category.
- 77 percent of the comments made about white football players fell into the Brains category, while only 22.5 percent of the comments about black players did so. The corresponding figures for basketball were 63 percent and 15 percent.

Margaret Duncan, Michael Messner, and Linda Williams (1990) studied the ways television commentators described athletes who participated in the 1989 NCAA women's and men's basketball finals and the 1989 women's and men's U.S. Open tennis tournaments. They found that commentators called female tennis players by their first rather than their full or last names 53 percent of the time, and men only 8 percent of the time. They also discovered that, of the men, only men of color were referred to by their first names only; full names were used to identify white male athletes. The researchers describe this overall pattern as a "hierarchy of naming," that is, a linguistic vehicle for reinforcing status differences between men and women, whites and blacks.

These studies suggest that racial stereotyping in sports media not only stirs up white supremacist sentiments and reinforces racist beliefs, but also shores up prevailing beliefs about the meaning of masculinity itself. As Ralph Ellison (1964) observed, "The object of the stereotype is not so much to crush the Negro as to console the white man."

BODY POLITICS OF RACE

White America has traditionally viewed black men in primarily physical terms. As Eldridge Cleaver (1967) asserted, whites used the myth of the black male as a "mindless supermasculine menial" to keep the slaves in their place and, later, to justify racial and occupational segregation. Ross Runfola (1980) argues that the adulation that highly successful black male athletes receive in white society not only encourages black males to "make it" with their bodies, but also allows whites to simultaneously block black men's access to the intellectual, political and economic sources of power and opportunity.

There is a political irony here. While the images of black men's bodies in sports media can empower the individual athlete, dissemination of these images in society at large may contribute to the collective emasculation and subjugation of black men. Black male athletes are extolled as manly men and good money-makers. Yet their immersion in the physical labor of sports reinforces supremacist assumptions that blacks are best suited to physical labor and not intellectual endeavors. In effect, media images of black men as physically adept and economically successful athletes tend to obscure blacks' and whites' historical relationship of oppression.

SOCIALLY STRUCTURED SILENCES

What is *not* said in sports media reveals as much or more about how gender and race politics unfold in the U.S. sports industry as what is said. A variety of socially structured silences surround black men in sports media. These silences cannot be explained as simple neglect or ghettoization of black male athletes. To the contrary, these silences are an integral part of the topography of American power relations.

Invisible Losers: Sports media do not ordinarily "cover" men who fail in sports or in life. Rather, they revel in those who succeed, or, for variation, in those athletes who have experienced failure in the form of injury, academic probation, drug addiction, incarceration, or delinquency, but who fight their way back to success. The has-beens, ne'er-do-wells, and quitters—in short, the real failures—seldom make the papers. "Rags to riches" stories in sports media far outnumber the "riches to rags" stories, like that of Henry Carr, a two-time gold-medal winner in the 1964 Summer Olympics and former defensive football captain of the New York Giants, who retired because of knee injuries, to eventually obtain employment as a janitor and car cleaner for a dealer in Griffin, Georgia. And the spotlight seldom shines on the approximately 60 percent of the NCAA Division I scholarship athletes in football and basketball who fail to graduate after five years of college (Eitzen 1987; Molotsky 1989).

Physical injuries or diminished abilities often cut down many male athletes of color at a relatively early age. Even those who do succeed for a while in sports find that the social and economic rewards slip through their fingers upon retirement. Without any marketable skills or, for many, a formal education to fall back on, the final scenario is all too familiar for the really unfortunate ones: i.e., substance abuse, irregular employment, downward mobility and sometimes prison (Melnick and Sabo, 1993).

Invisible Injuries: Exploitative institutions pull people in, chew them up, and, when the people have lost their usefulness, spit them out again. For every young hero valorized on the screen, hundreds, perhaps thousands, of former athletes live with chronic pain and disability that result from injuries sustained during their "playing" days. In sports media, however, injury is often portrayed as a mark of manhood, a temporary obstacle for an athlete to overcome, or an unusual, unforeseen tragedy.

Injury is everywhere and nowhere in sports. The ubiquity of sports injury is evident in the lives and bodies of athletes who frequently experience bruises, torn ligaments, broken bones, aches, lacerations and muscle tears. Three hundred thousand football-related injuries per year require treatment in hospital emergency rooms. Yet sports media ignore the toll that sports injuries take on the bodies, psyches, and lives of male athletes.

Some of the gender and racial dimensions behind the media silences surrounding sports injury can be seen in recent portrayals of Muhammed Ali. On March 1, 1992, a two-hour-long tribute to the former boxer and "heavyweight champion of the world" was televised. A cavalcade of big-name celebrities combined their talent and popularity to create "Muhammed Ali's Fiftieth Birthday Celebration." Beneath the glamor of the production, and behind Ali's very real athletic accomplishments, however, there lurked the reality that Ali has become severely disabled by a form of Parkinson's Disease caused by the repeated trauma his brain sustained in the ring. During the show Ali had difficulty shaking hands, and when he tried to raise his arms above his head as a gesture of unity with the applauding audience, he could not fully extend his arms. His speech was slurred, and at one point he strained to clap his hands but could not complete the movement. Ali's life as a rebel, a war protester, a Muslim minister, and a boisterous opponent of racism was rewritten via big-stage production numbers. Ali the victim was transformed into Ali the hero. Ignored was the fact that, ultimately, boxing had reduced Ali "the Greatest" to a stumbling, brain-damaged, middle-aged rich man who smiles into the cameras that follow and frame him.

Presence without Power: Blacks make up 60 percent of players in professional football, 70 percent in professional basketball, and 17 percent in professional baseball, and many participate in Olympic and intercollegiate sports. The high visibility of successful black men in sports fosters the impression that sports provide upward social mobility for African Americans. This impression, however, is not supported by the facts. The probability of an African American or other man of color gaining mobility through a professional sports career is extremely low. Only three thousand athletes, altogether, participate in major-league baseball, the National Basketball Association (NBA), the NFL, and professional boxing. Probably no more than twelve hundred African American and one hundred fifty other men of color play these professional sports in the United States today.

The image of the male athlete as celebrity is created, cultivated and amplified by the sports media. Whether black or white, the celebrity athlete exemplifies the self-fulfilled man who has won success, recognition and occupational achievement in the competitive and risk-laden American economy. Yet, because of racism, the successes of black and white athletes are perceived differently among class and racial subgroups. For example, bigoted whites, whose racial prejudices make them prone to overgeneralization about blacks, may be led to assume that black men in general are faring better in the American economy than they really are.

Though blacks are generally more skeptical in their appraisals of opportunity and social mobility, many working-class and poor black males see sports as a way to prove their manhood and as a pathway out of the ghetto. Only a few, of course, achieve the dream while the majority continue to contend with the poverty and discrimination. Leonard and Reyman (1988) calculated the odds of a twenty- to thirty-nine-year-old African American male getting to play in the NFL at 1 in 47,600, an eighteen- to thirty-nine-year-old black man getting to play major-league baseball at 1 in 333,000, and a twenty- to thirty-nine-year-old getting to play in the NBA at 1 in 153,800. (For Hispanic males in the same age ranges, the respective odds are 1 in 2,500,000, 1 in 500,000 and 1 in 33,300,000.)

Though men of color are statistically overrepresented among professional athletes, they are very much underrepresented among coaches (only 7 percent of NFL and NBA coaches are men of color), managers (only 11 percent in major-league baseball are men of color), and front-office staff (8 to 14 percent are men of color) (Braddock 1989; Lapchick and Brown 1992). Despite the high percentages of athletes in these sports who belong to racial or ethnic minorities, minority representation among nonathletes in professional sports is disproportionately low.

Back of the Broadcasting Bus: Black sports journalists and radio and television commentators are also scarce commodities. Those who exist are more apt to be found on the sidelines or hanging around the locker-room door than co-anchoring with the middle-aged white men who prevail behind the microphones. The few blacks who do make it as TV and radio sports commentators usually adhere to established editorial policies and standard journalistic practices; and, except for rare special assignments, racial issues are not part of the sports reporter's beat. For example, sports commentators expressed no solidarity with Native American protests at games played by the Washington Redskins throughout the 1991 to 1992 football season; moreover, this silence prevailed in spite of the fact that some black players supported the Native American position (Lewis 1992).

The high media visibility of stars such as Magic Johnson contributes to the myth that sport is a vehicle for young African American males to achieve upward mobility. In fact, there are only about 1200 African American and 150 other men of color playing the main pro sports in the U.S. today.

MARKETING HEROES AND DEMONS

It is "business as usual" that keeps most black athletes in the back pages of the newspapers and away from the microphones and media markets. When black athletes do receive significant individual coverage, usually they are in sports that reinforce the old stereotype of black men as big, bad brutes (like sack-monster Reggie White), or they are embroiled in scandal (like Ben Johnson who used steroids), or, as in the case of Magic Johnson, their behavior away from the game imperils their performance or career. Seldom do we find sports media describing the intelligence, hard work, and discipline that are necessary for black (as well as white) athletes to produce peak performances. More often, sports media perpetuate the racist assumption that blacks who excel physically are just doing what comes naturally for them.

Sometimes media reports of sport scandals have racist overtones, such as in the case of Sugar Ray Leonard's drug abuse and wife-beating or Mike Tyson's rape trial as Messner and Solomon discuss in Chapter 2 of this book. Over several days' time, the media shifted focus from Sugar Ray Leonard as a battering husband to Leonard as a retired champion struggling to come back after a bout with drug abuse, thus diverting attention from the larger issue of men's violence against women and, more specifically, male violence in the black community.

Sportswriters examined "Iron Mike" Tyson's transgression from different angles—to explore precedents from the history of sport, to discuss Tyson's unsuitability for boxing, to analyze the athlete's life in and out of the gym, to review the legal implications of the case, to point out that Tyson was young and image-conscious, and so on (Saraceno 1991). The media gave the case so much coverage, of course, to attract the readers with "hot"—sensational and therefore very marketable—copy.

Giving Tyson so much attention, however, made him seem to be an anomaly, whether as cheat, imposter, or tragic victim of flawed judgment, or as a compulsive personality. By demonizing Tyson as a deviant hulk, the links between hegemonic masculinity, sexism, sports and violence against women remained hidden between the lines.

SOME CHANGES

Media stories about black male athletes are often framed in positive ways. Television coverage of athletic events often includes portraits of athletes that show them engaged in community work (these portraits are often done in conjunction with public relations plugs; for example, "The NFL supports the United Way in your community"). Similarly, coverage of intercollegiate athletic events sometimes highlights the academic achievements of black student-athletes by depicting them in laboratories or walking across campus with books in hand. These images do not say as much about athletes' lives and struggles in a racist society as they do about the image the NCAA or its university co-sponsors are trying to establish. Still, these images represent a move away from racial stereotypes and traditional portrayals of male athletes.

The grievances we have compiled here indicate that sports media play integral, not ancillary, roles in the larger social and cultural processes that perpetuate white men's domination over black men, and men's domination over women. Nevertheless, producers of sports media are becoming more conscious about the way they portray people. In some cases, they are not only working to eliminate racism from media, they are also projecting positive images of black men.

These moves may in part be responses to criticism from educators and activists, like the late Arthur Ashe, who deplored unrealistic, one-dimensional media representations of athletes as role models for young black males. Production of these positive images is also a pragmatic response by media organizations to the changing demographics of network television audiences, who are less white and less affluent than before.

Though the media moguls may be making these moves more because they have seen the numbers than because they have seen the light, they are still moves in the right direction.

REFERENCES

Braddock II, J. H. 1989., "Sport and Race Relations in American Society." *Sociological Symposium* 9:53-76.

Cleaver, E. 1967. *Soul on Ice*. New York: McGraw-Hill.

Duncan, M. C., M. A. Messner, and L. Williams. 1990. Gender Stereotyping in Televised Sports. Los Angeles: Amateur Athletic Foundation.

Ellison, R. 1964. *Shadow and Act*. New York: Random House.

Eitzen, S. D. 1987. "The Educational Experiences of Intercollegiate Student-Athletes." *Journal Sport and Social Issues* 11(2):111-35 .

Fanon, F. 1970. *Black Skins, White Masks*. London: Paladin.

Jackson, D. Z. 1989. "Calling the Plays in Black and White." *Boston Globe*, January 22.

Lapchick, R. E., and J. P. Brown. 1992. "Do Professional Sports Provide Equal Opportunities for All Races?" *1992 Racial Report Card* 4(#2:1):4-9. Boston: Northeastern University Center for the Study of Sport in Society.

Leonard, W. M., II, and J. E. Reyman. 1988. "The Odds of Attaining Professional Athlete Status: Refining the Computations." *Sociology of Sport Journal* 5:162-69.

Lewis, C. 1992. "The Shy Kid Who Came to Visit Is More than a Football Hero." *The Philadelphia Inquirer*, January 29.

Malee, M. 1992. "Patriotic Symbols in Intercollegiate Sports During the Persian Gulf War." Unpublished paper, Department of Sociology, Boston College.

Melnick, M., and D. Sabo. 1993. "Sport and Social Mobility among African-American and Hispanic Athletes." In *Ethnic Experiences in North American Sport*, ed. G. Eisen and D. Wiggins. Westport, CT: Greenwood Press.

Molotsky, L. 1989. "Graduation Rate of Athletes Below 20 Percent at Many Schools." *The New York Times*, September 10.

Rainville, R. E., and E. McCormick. 1977. "Extent of Covert Racial Prejudice in Pro Football Announcers' Speech." *Journalism Quarterly*. 54(1):20-6.

Runfola, R. 1980. "The Black Athlete as Super-Machismo Symbol." In *Jock: Sports and Male Identity*, ed. D. F. Sabo and R. Runfola, 79-88. Englewood Cliffs, NJ: Prentice-Hall.

Saraceno, J. 1991. "Tyson Indicted." *USA Today*, September 10.

Weisman, J. 1992. "Sundays, Bloody Sundays: Pro Football—The Maiming Game." *The Nation* 254(3):84, 86-7.

Doing Time Doing Masculinity: Sports and Prison

DON SABO

I am a white male college professor in my forties hunched over a desk in Attica Correctional Facility. My heart is pounding, my upper body is taut and shaking, and I am gazing into the eyes of an African-American prisoner who, like so many of the men in this New York state prison, comes from what sociologists call the underclass. We are different in most respects, but right now we are alike. Like me, he's puffing and straining, trying not to show it, sometimes cursing, and returning my gaze. We are arm wrestling. He puts me down after about two minutes, which, in arm wrestling, can be a long, long time.

I started arm wrestling in the joint, as I like to call it, about five years ago. I enjoy the physical connection with other men that the contest allows. The participants initially stalk one another over a period of days or weeks, keeping their distance, evaluating each other's strengths and weaknesses. Playful badmouthing or boasting may lead to a bout. Eventually they make the necessary moves that bring each to the table, hand in hand, eye to eye. Even though arm wrestling is combative, it can foster a closer connection with another man that is not allowed for in most aspects of men's lives. Arm wrestling here allows me to climb outside the bourgeois husk of my life and join with somebody in a way that temporarily suspends the hierarchical distinctions between free man and inmate, white and black, privileged and underprivileged, and teacher and student.

Arm wrestling also lets me pull my athletic past into the present, to enjoin youthful masculine spirits and facades. At the same time that these manly juices start flowing again, though, I tell myself and others that I don't take the competition seriously. I want to learn that it is OK to be vulnerable to defeat.

Sometimes I win, sometimes I lose. It still matters to me whether I win or lose. I try hard to win, but, when I lose, I get over it quickly; I accept my loss and even welcome it as inevitable. Part of me is happy for the man who has beaten me. When I win, I savor the victory for a few days, bragging to myself, sometimes to others, soothing my middle-aged ego with the transparent rationalization that I'm still strong, not over the bloody hill yet. Arm wrestlers understand that nobody wins all the time. Beneath the grit and show, we know there is more to the game than winning or losing. We also know that part of what makes arm wrestling more than just a contest or pastime is that it somehow speaks to our beliefs and feelings about being men.

I have taught in prisons for fourteen years.* My experiences, observations, and discussions with inmates have revealed that prison

*For more about men, prison, and gender issues, see Don Sabo and Willie London's "Men in Prison: A Special Issue" (*Men's Studies Review* 9(1), 1992). More than one million men are imprisoned in American jails and prisons. The United States has the highest rate of incarceration of any nation in the world, followed by South Africa and the Soviet Union. Men of color are statistically overrepresented among those behind bars. Black and Hispanic males, for example, make up 85 percent of prisoners in the New York state prison system. The estimated cost of incarcerating all the prisoners in the United States is $16 billion per year. If the state prison population continued to grow at the same pace as it did during 1989, that level of growth would require "building the equivalent of a 1000-bed prison every 6 days," according to P. A. Langan (America's soaring prison population, *Science* 251 [March 1991] 1568-73).

sports mean different things to different men. I have learned that a great many motives, messages, and contradictions are crammed into the muscles and athletic pastimes of men in prison. Like men outside the walls, prisoners use sports for creating and maintaining their masculine identities.

DOING TIME DOING SPORTS

Perhaps the most striking aspect of prison sports is their visibility. The yard is the hub of athletic activity. Weight lifters huddle in small groups around barbells and bench press racks. Runners circle the periphery, while hoopsters spin and shoot on the basketball courts. There is the occasional volleyball game or bocce tournament. Depending on the facility and time of year, there may be football practices or games, replete with equipment and fans along the sidelines. Some prisons have softball leagues and diamonds.

Inside the buildings are a gym, basketball courts, and weight rooms. Powerlifters struggle against gravity and insanity. Feats of strength produce heroes in the joint, sometimes even legends (local legends, at least). I have been told stories about Jihad Al-Sibbar, a man past his forties who weighs 155 pounds. He is believed to be the strongest man in the New York state prison system; I've heard it said more than once that, if given the opportunity, he could have competed in the Olympics. I want and need to believe these stories, not so much because they are tales of a strong man, but because his triumphs say something about the potential of athletics to sustain sanity in an insane place.

Sports and fitness activities spill into the prison environment in other ways. An inmate may do daily calisthenics while in solitary. Martin Sostre, an African-American black power activist and inner-city bookstore owner who was framed by police in 1967 and imprisoned for nine years, used yoga and other physical exercise to survive long stints of solitary confinement and to strengthen himself for his political struggles against prison and legal authorities.*

*Sostre's struggles were described to me by sociologist Elwin Powell, who studied the Sostre case for many years and advocated his release. See also The Crime of Martin Sostre, by Vincent Copeland (New York: McGraw Hill, 1970).

In almost any part of the prison, sports fans may jabber about who will win the superbowl, the NBA finals, or the next heavyweight boxing match. The taunting, teasing, and betting that typifies sports fans outside the walls is also rife among inmates, guards, and personnel. Men gather in groups around television sets to watch the Final Four or Monday Night Football, while others sit alone in their cells jabbing with George Foreman or soaring with Michael Jordan.

Sports and fitness activities in prison engage men's minds and bodies to varying degrees and, in the process, help them do their time. For some men, especially the young ones, athletics are no more than a fleeting pastime, a form of physical play, something to do to get to the end of another day. For others, sports and fitness activities are a survival strategy, a regimen for maintaining physical and mental health in a hostile, unhealthful place. Still others work out or play sports to dispel anger and frustration, to get the rage out of their bodies and psyches before it explodes or turns in on them. And there are those who get big to be bad, who develop muscle and a jock presence to intimidate and dominate others.

DOING MASCULINITY

The prison environment triggers a masculine awareness in me. I go on masculine alert. I don't walk around with biceps flexed and chest expanded, pretending to be a tough guy for anybody looking my way. That kind of suck-in-your-belly-and-lower-your-voice stuff faded away with my twenties. The masculinity that surfaces in the prison is more of an attitude, a hazy cluster of concerns and expectations that get translated into emotion and physical movement in ways that never quite come clear. Though there are a few women around (for example, an occasional female guard, some female teachers), I see and smell the prison as an all-male domain. I sense a potential for danger, and I feel a heightened need to protect myself. I could get caught in a bad situation. I have been told not to trust anybody—prisoners, guards, or bureaucrats. Nobody. It sounds crazy, but the distrust almost feels good. Indeed, there are parts of me, call them "threads" or "echoes" of an old masculine identity, that embrace the distrust and welcome the presumed danger and potential for violence.

This masculine awareness is seldom uppermost in my mind. It does not emanate from inside of me, but, rather, it is more like a visitor who comes and goes, moving in and out of me like tap water gushing in and out of an overfilled glass. Arm wrestling allows me to play out masculinity in tune with other elements of jailhouse jock culture. At the same time, the wrestling breeds familiarity with prisoners, pushes us toward closeness and trust, and subverts hierarchical distinctions based on class, race, and professional status.

Like me, many men in prison use sports and exercise to "do" masculinity—that is, to spin masculine identities, build reputations, to achieve or dissolve status. For the men in prison, as elsewhere, masculine identity is earned, enacted, rehearsed, refined, and relived through each day's activities and choices. I'm not saying that the gender roles men follow in prison are reinvented each day, from moment to moment, man to man. Masculinity does not unfold inside us as much as it flows through us. It is not a strictly individual or psychological process. In "doing" masculinity, each man participates in the larger prison culture, which scripts masculinity by supplying direction, role models, props, motivations, rewards, and values.* For many men, sports are a part of the formula for shaping gender identity.

SOFTNESS AND HARDNESS

In prison, the manly injunction to be strong is not only evident in the bulk and bearing of many men's bodies, but in everyday speech as well. I have often heard prisoners describe other men as "hard" or "soft." Over the years, I have learned that there are many guises of hardness, which, inside and outside the prison culture, illustrate various ways of expressing masculinity from the honorable to the perverse.

*For an interesting discussion of masculinity as a "situated accomplishment," see James W. Messerschmidt's *Masculinities and Crime: Critique and Reconceptualization of Theory* (Lanham, MD: Lanham and Littlefield, 1993). Additional writings on "doing gender" include Candace West and Don H. Zimmerman's "Doing Gender" (*Gender and Society* 1(2):125-51, 1987) and Todd Crosset's *Out Here: Sport and Gender on the Women's Professional Golf Tour* (Albany, NY: State University of New York Press).

Being hard can mean that the individual is toned, strong, conditioned, fit—not weak, flabby, or out of shape. A hard man cares for and respects his body. It is extraordinarily difficult to eke out a healthful lifestyle here. Cigarette smoke is everywhere. The noise on the blocks can jam the senses. The chow stinks, as inmates say; a nutritionally sound diet is impossible to establish from the available cafeteria fare. For some men, then, playing sports and exercising constitute a personal quest to develop a healthy body in an unhealthful environment.

Some men strive to be hard as a way of building self-esteem, garnering the respect of others. Being in prison is a constant, colossal reminder of personal failure. A regular fitness regimen helps a man center his identity in the undeniably tangible locus of the body. Others find that getting good at basketball or being recognized as a leading athlete earns them the respect of peers. Damaged egos and healing psyches drink in the recognition and repair themselves.

Being hard can also be a defense against prison violence. The hard man sends the message that he is not a pushover, not somebody to "fuck with." The sexual connotations of this latter phrase take on particular significance in the prison subculture, where man-on-man rape is part of life. Prison rape serves to constitute intermale dominance hierarchies, which make up the web of male relations. Blacks may rape

In prison, developing a "hard body" can be a way of building healthy self esteem, and it can also serve as a defense against the omnipresent threat of violence.

whites in order to establish dominant status, or vice versa. Long-term prisoners may rape newcomers to enslave them. Guards or prison administrators have been known to threaten to expose prisoners to greater threat of rape in order to evoke good behavior, to punish, or to squeeze out information. As Tom Cahill (1990, 32), himself a victim of prison rape, observed,

> Once "turned out"—prison parlance for raped—a survivor is caught in a bind. If an inmate reports a sexual assault, even without naming the assailant, he will be labeled a "snitch," a contract will automatically be placed on him, and his life expectancy will be measured in minutes from then.

It would be a mistake, however, to perceive prison rape mainly as a power dynamic of intermale dominance hierarchies. Inmates' struggles to dominate one another through rape and physical intimidation reflect and reproduce men's domination of women in the social world beyond the walls. In the muscled, violent, and tattooed world of the prison, woman is symbolically ever-present. She resides in the pulpy, supple, and muted linguistic folds of the hardness-softness dichotomy. The prison phrase "make a woman out of you" means that the person who is addressed will be raped. Rape-based relationships between prisoners are often described as relations between "men" and "girls"—or "masters" and "slaves," victors and vanquished.

The hardness-softness dichotomy echoes and fortifies stereotypes of masculinity and femininity. To be "hard" means being more manly than the next guy, who is said to be "soft" and more feminine. To be called hard is a compliment; to be labeled soft can be a playful chide or a serious put-down. The connotations around hardness and softness also flow from and feed homophobia, which is rampant in prison. The stigma of being labeled a homosexual can make a man more vulnerable to ridicule, attack, and ostracism.

When I arm-wrestle in prison, I am waist-deep in contradiction. Prison somehow magnifies contradiction, making it palpable, visible. The scripts of softness and hardness collide in my face. Although I seek human connection and fun, the contest creates a winner and a loser. No matter how far I reach across the table toward men from different social and racial backgrounds, my white face and professorial status stretch with me. The other men remain prisoners and I remain the professor. In spite of these contradictions, I still feel that the men I teach and wrestle with are like me: they are trying to figure out what is going on in their lives, and that part of this struggle hinges on understanding masculinity.

For many prisoners, the pursuit of manhood has presented another contradiction. James Messerschmidt (1993) shows how some men use crime to construct masculine identities, to "do masculinity". To be good providers for their families, they join gangs in hopes of becoming "big men" in the street; they become "badasses" or "gangsters" to get respect from peers; they brave the violence of the drug trade; they rape or beat women to prove manly superiority; or they embezzle their way to financial success and masculine adequacy. The irony is that these quests for manly power often lead to incarceration—to a loss of the freedom and dignity a manly life requires. For many prisoners, and for countless men on the outside, following well-worn pathways to masculinity turned out to be a trap.

Inherent in men's participation in prison sports is yet another contradiction. For inmates, sports and exercise are vehicles for self-expression and physical freedom. For prison officials, inmates' involvement in sports and exercise helps make them more tractable. Hence, the development of the prisoner's body through sports and exercise activities is simultaneously a source of personal liberation and a tool for social control.

It is easy for men in prison, or on the outside, to get trapped by the overarching cultural mandate of hardness. The image of the male athlete as muscled, aggressive, competitive, and emotionally controlled dovetails with the prevailing definition of masculinity in sexist culture.

Conformity to this model of manliness can be socially and emotionally destructive.

Muscles may remain "*the* sign of masculinity" in the culture of intermale dominance hierarchies that characterize the U.S. prison system (Glassner 1988). And yet my observations tell me that prisoners' attitudes toward muscle and masculinity are varying and complex. Whereas for some men conformity to the credo of hardness feeds the forces of domination and subordination, for others athletics and exercise are forms of self-care. While many prison jocks are playing out the masculine roles they learned in their youth, others are attempting to use sports and exercise to promote health, sanity, and alternative modes of masculinity.

Perhaps the greatest contradiction pervading prison sports is that, despite the diversity of meanings that prisoners attach to their bodies through sports and exercise, the cultural mandate for hardness and toughness prevails. Men's soft sides remain hidden. The punitive and often violent prison hierarchies persist, breathing aggression and fear into men's bodies and minds, in spite of those who seek softer ways of being men. The same tragic contradiction informs men's lives in sport outside the prison walls, where gender inequality and sexism constrain efforts to improve relations between the sexes and attitudes about the human body.

In the end, arm wrestling allows me to squeeze new meanings of masculinity from the grip of political and cultural contradiction. I learn that the cages in men's lives can be made of iron bars, muscles, or myths. The harder I wrestle, the more I dream of escape.

REFERENCES

Cahill, Tom. 1990. "Prison Rape: Torture in the American Gulag." In *Men and Intimacy: Personal Accounts Exploring the Dilemmas of Modern Male Sexuality*, ed. Franklin Abbott. Freedom, CA: The Crossing Press.

Glassner, Barry. 1988. *Bodies: Why We Look the Way We Do (and How We Feel about It)*. New York: Putnam.

Messerschmidt, James W. 1993. *Masculinities and Crime: Critique and Reconceptualization of Theory*. Lanham, MD: Lanham and Littlefield.

Part VI

CHANGING SPORTS, CHANGING MEN

Men's lives today are very different from those of our parents or grandparents. Once buttressed by custom and law, male authority in family, religion, and government has progressively eroded—as well it should. Women have struggled for much of this change under the banner of equal opportunity, and feminists continue to push for economic and political parity with men.

Men, too, are waking up and realizing that the world of gender relations has changed around them. While some men still cling to conventional definitions of masculinity and femininity, others are dissatisfied with what they sense are outmoded, awkward, and self-destructive norms for masculine behavior. Many want to change their lives, but either are unsure of exactly what the problem is or don't know where to begin.

We put this book together to encourage men and women to rethink, redefine, and reshape their identities, relationships, and the social structures in which they live. The analysis of sport is a good place to begin creating a new map for the future of masculinity. A lot of men have played sports or they've been fans all their lives. Even men who hate sports and are turned off by the whole jock image are still hooked in because they hate it.

Two of the essays in this section draw on feminist theories and ideas in order to talk about changing masculinity and sports. The words feminist and feminism must be among the most misunderstood words in U.S. society. We understand feminism and feminist theory simply as efforts to understand and change women's and men's lives in more humane and egalitarian directions. Feminists envision a future in which men and women work together as equals rather than living lives at cross-purposes.

One place for men to begin changing is in their experience of their bodies. Sports are a theater for physical expression and experimentation. In the past, men's experiences of their bodies and exercise have been structured by the notions about masculinity that prevailed in institutionalized competitive sports. These beliefs often glorified pain and injury, and emphasized stoic denial, and blocked men's experience of mind-body unity. Somewhere in history, the appreciation for health, fun, and bodily pleasure in men's sports got buried underneath the locker-room tiles. Gym classes and sports teams were modeled after the military boot camp experience, resulting in a militarization of the everyday life of men's bodies. By redefining the relations between masculinity and sports, men may not only discover new ways of knowing and experiencing their bodies, but they might also enhance their body awareness and health.

Participation in mixed-sex athletics is another way for men to change the sports/masculinity connection. The walls of sex segregation in sports have been crumbling in recent decades. We now have children's baseball leagues, adult softball teams, school intramural programs, racket sports, private health clubs, running, weight lifting, and volleyball open to both sexes. The experience of mixed-sex athletics can help men not only to learn to cooperate with and compete as equals against women, but also to discover potentialities in themselves that may have been suppressed in male-dominated sports.

Working for gender equity in athletics is another way men can transform masculinity and sexist practices. Whether to give girls and women the same fair shake at playing high-school and intercollegiate sports as boys and men has until recently been viewed as a "women's issue." Equal allocation of athletic resources and opportunities would certainly do good things for women, but boys and men also have much to gain from the changes that gender equity would bring to sports.

Discussions about gender equity in sports often force us to ask fundamental questions about the kind of athletic experiences we want to create for ourselves and society. What values should sports engender? What character traits do we want to nurture in our athletes? When Canadian track and field star Ben Johnson tested positive for steroids during the 1988 Summer Olympics, his fellow citizens were initially shocked and dismayed. Ben Johnson got slammed by the media and ostracized from formal competition. Eventually, however, many sport leaders realized that the real significance behind the "Ben Johnson scandal" was not so much his personal tragedy, but that his cheating and drug abuse were part of a widespread erosion of the traditional Canadian commitment to sport as a promoter of physical health, fair competition, and character development.

Similarly, the assault on figure skater Nancy Kerrigan in the winter of 1994 sent a wake-up call to many American sport leaders who are concerned that the commercialization of athletics and the "winning is everything" mentality are undermining the educational and healthful purposes of sports in the United States. The key question surrounding the "Tonya Harding scandal" is not her guilt or innocence, or whether some women athletes are becoming as corrupted as some men athletes. Rather, the central issue is whether the values and practices of American sports are becoming so distorted by excessive competition that the health and character of *both* men and women athletes are being jeopardized. In several of the essays to follow, we try to show how pursuing gender equity in athletics will help make sports a more healthful institution for both sexes.

It is not enough for men to understand sexism. We have to fight it, too, and in so doing attempt to change the institutions that perpetuate it. Toward this end, we have provided a list of strategies for men to consider as they attempt to transform themselves, sports, and society.

Getting Beyond Exercise as Work

DON SABO

Exercise is intrinsic to the jock culture. Work and sports have been central proving grounds of masculinity, and both serve as arenas for competition and combative camaraderie. They determine a male's sense of mastery or failure and engender feelings of superiority to women. Work and sports are underpinned by the same ethos of success, potency, and prestige. The self-made man theme is shared by the Horatio Alger stories and tales of successful jocks from John L. Sullivan to former president Gerald Ford. Moreover, work and sports similarly shape the male personality and generate such traits as independence, ambitiousness, dominance, emotional detachment, and competitiveness. Like certain jobs, many sports are traditionally considered masculine; they endow men with a sense of self-denial and an aura of toughness and ruthlessness deemed necessary to achieve success. This constellation of character traits implies an active and instrumental attitude—

one that emphasizes conquest, competitive skills, and a preoccupation with the end results of activity.

Considerable overlap, then, has existed between the work ethic and the male approach to exercise. To put it simply, men have defined and experienced exercise as work. The term workout, used to describe an afternoon at the gym or a calisthenics session, illustrates this identification. Men usually approach exercise with ascetic rigor and purpose. They accept varying degrees of physical pain and sweaty exhaustion as essential to the process. Competition is also an integral part of the activity, whether the individual competes against others or against himself. And the expected end products of exercise uppermost in the exerciser's mind are a better physique, health, muscular development, or sexual vitality. The mind regards the body as an object to be moved, manipulated, and developed in order to achieve desired results. The body is treated as a machine to be set in motion or an obstacle to be surmounted rather than an organic part of the self. The notion that exercise is or can be pleasurably sensuous is alien to the jock ethos.

GETTING BEYOND EXERCISE AS WORK: A NON-JOCK APPROACH

When involved with the work ethic, exercise fosters the development of traditional masculine character traits that, in turn, help to maintain sexist attitudes and social relations. A small step might be taken toward women's and men's liberation by redefining exercise in a nonsexist way. Such a non-jock approach to exercise would be predicated upon the pleasure principle and not on the glorification of strenuous physical toil. Sensual enjoyment would replace ascetic self-denial. The body would be perceived organically and not mechanically. Consciousness would focus upon immediate physical sensations, not on visions of future rewards. The exerciser would passively participate in the bodily process rather than attempting to control it.

BODY-AWARENESS EXERCISES: TUNING IN TO BODY

The following exercises are designed to induce new states of body awareness and to move consciousness away from traditional masculine attitudes. Each exercise can be done alone or in a group. Above all, try not to approach the exercises as a crusade for self-improvement. Crusades end up being work. A passive approach is more likely to result in a sense of self-improvement.

Body Fantasies: Masculine identity is a social product. The individual male has learned to perceive and interpret bodily sensations from within a masculine self-concept. The first two exercises promote mild alterations in everyday consciousness; through these changes in consciousness you can experience changes in body awareness. The mind beckons and the body follows. Restructuring our fantasies lets us perceive sensory input in new ways, so we can gently replace old, culturally conditioned, perceptions with an organismic sensitivity.Each fantasy exercise should be carried out in a relaxed position. Sit comfortably, or lie down on the floor or a couch. Keep your eyes closed.

1. *The ideal body fantasy.* Think of your mind as an empty movie theater. You are seated in the front row. Before you is a large movie screen. Visualize a male body on the screen that you would like for your own. If you could live inside another body, the body on the screen would be your ideal choice. Picture the body walking, swimming, or moving freely about a room. Imagine how it would feel to be inside such a body. Focus on your immediate physical sensations. Let yourself feel them for a minute or two. Think about them.

   Now, slowly visualize the screen going black. You are alone again, back in your own body, in a totally dark theater. Become aware of your breathing. Feel the positioning of your neck, head, and arms. Now take your hands and explore the contours of your face. Touch your cheeks, chest, and stomach. Stroke your legs and grip your knees. Be thankful for your body. Regard it as a gift. Contemplate its wonders. When you are ready, slowly open your eyes.

2. *The holding in your belly fantasy.* Once again, you are in a darkened movie theater. This time, however, visualize yourself upon the screen. Picture yourself in a situation in which you are scantily clad and self-conscious about your body. Perhaps you are at a beach or undressing before a lover. Think about your self-consciousness. How concerned are you about other people's eyes? How do you cover up your embarrassment? How does it feel? Try to determine the bodily tensions you are experiencing. Are you holding your belly in? Is your chest out? Are you tensely conscious of your posture?

   Again, let the screen go black. You are alone in your body. Focus on your breathing. Locate any stiffness or tension you feel. Is it in your neck? Your lower back or abdomen? Now direct each exhalation of your breath to the locus of the tension. Imagine that, with each exhalation, the tension is gradually dissipating. Be conscious of any signs of increased relaxation. When you feel relaxed, open your eyes.

Stretching Exercises: Most adult bodies are stiff. Our bodies are too frequently the reluctant vehicles of consciousness. While one suffers from disuse, the fluidity of another is impeded by an overdeveloped musculature. The body is perceived as a constraint, an alien object to be overcome and pushed forward. Hence, the jock phrase "pushing yourself" means ordering the body about against its will.

The instrumental orientation of the masculine character is exemplified in the jock approach to stretching exercises. They are a preparatory endeavor. They are done to get ready for a physical challenge or to avoid a torn muscle. The body-machine must function well and respond to commands. When a jock stretches, he is punching a time clock to begin work.

The non-jock approach to stretching exercises stresses the unity of mind and body. Relaxation is the mind-set. Here, the body beckons and the mind follows. Only two stretching exercises are described below, but you can easily use the ideas presented here to invent others.

1. *The sun-reach*. Stand comfortably with your hands at your side. Become conscious of your breathing. Focusing upon your physical sensations, slowly raise both arms above your head. Think about the experience while it is happening. What is occurring in your body? Next, stretch your hands skyward as far as possible. Don't strain. Feel your spine stretch upward. What happens to your sense of balance? Now, lower your arms to their original position. Look for a sense of relaxation. Repeat the exercise several times.

2. *The leg and back stretch*. Stand with your legs far apart. Focus on your breathing. Slowly bend forward from the hips, and stretch your hands toward the floor at a point midway between your feet. What are you feeling, and where? Listen to your body making adjustments to maintain balance. Get into that balance. Let yourself relax. Let your arms hang. Slowly stand upright again. Look for a sense of relaxation. Repeat this exercise as often as desired or whenever you feel fatigued or stiff.

Slow-motion calisthenics: Calisthenics are seldom done for pleasure. Fitness is the usual aim. Fear of unfitness is often the motive. Calisthenics are performed mechanically and dutifully. Each repetition is counted, and the tally denotes the degree of achievement.

Non-jock calisthenics wed awareness with physical motion. Fitness is a by-product, not the aim. The idea is to explore the body, not to discipline it. Mind and body dance. Counting repetitions is needless.

The focus is upon bodily cues and processes. The types of non-jock calisthenics are innumerable, so feel free to try others as well as the two described as follows.

1. *Rolling the arms.* With your eyes closed, stand comfortably with your arms extended straight out sideways. Be aware of your breathing. Think of a reason you are glad to be alive. Slowly begin moving both arms in small circles. Focus upon your arm muscles and the movements of your shoulder joints. What are you feeling? Progressively increase the size of the circles. Let your mind follow the body's movements. Slowly decrease the size of the circles until your arms return to their original position. The exercise may be repeated and speeded up but not to the extent that your sense of unity with the body's motion is disturbed.

2. *Pushing.* Lie face down on the floor in the pushup position. Breathe as slowly as is comfortable, and relax. Allow your body to go limp. Think of yourself as a child asleep on its belly. Next, very slowly, begin to push yourself upward. Feel your arm muscles tense. Feel the weight of your body. How is your breathing? Your arms should eventually be straightened. What emotions are you experiencing? Do you feel light or heavy, strong or weak? Begin lowering your body toward the floor. Embrace the motion. Rest when you are finished. Repeat the exercise as often as you wish, but avoid straining yourself. Be aware of your body's strengths and limitations.

THE NON-JOCK APPROACH TO EXERCISE AND WOMEN'S AND MEN'S LIBERATION

The jock approach to exercise, so tied to the work ethic, encourages the formation and preservation of traditional masculine personality traits. Moreover, athletics reinforce the alienated, instrumental, and objectified relation between a man's consciousness and his body. The average male perceives his body as a thing to be stoically ignored or controlled rather than an organismic part of himself. Research indicates that males are less aware of their bodies than females, less sensitive to bodily cues (Fisher 1974). As culture conditions consciousness, the body becomes the vehicle of identity, which, in turn, shapes the self-concept. The body contains the history of its social origins. Mind, body, and society ceaselessly interact. The biosocial wheel turns onward. Hence, traditional masculinity and sexism are organically as well as socially perpetuated.

The non-jock approach to exercise attempts to help men move from beneath the biosocial wheel by discovering and deriving pleasure from bodily sensations and to restructure consciousness away from traditional masculinity. Wilhelm Reich's character analytic framework illustrates the potential of the non-jock approach to exercise to provide sensual enjoyment and changes in character. Reich conceives of the body as the structural embodiment of character. A paranoiac, for example, may appear guarded and rigidly defensive in posture and facial expression. An individual's social and emotional history is usually embedded in his or her musculature and nervous system. Reich describes the mannerisms, patterns of speech, postures, and motions by which an individual manages inner tensions and wards off threats from the outside world. Reich's therapeutic technique is to repeatedly call attention to an undesirable character trait and compel the patient to experience the mannerism associated with it. The patient's heightened awareness of the trait leads to its eventual disappearance and thus to improved psychic health (Reich 1972; Boadella 1974).

The body-fantasy exercises described in this chapter are consistent with Reich's theory in that they enable you to explore bodily sensations in various imagined psychosocial contexts. In this way you learn to make conscious connections between certain bodily states and corresponding masculine images and roles. One moment you visualize and experience your body in a social role; the next moment, you are your body. The stretching exercises and slow-motion calisthenics are also intended to enhance your body awareness and induce mind-body

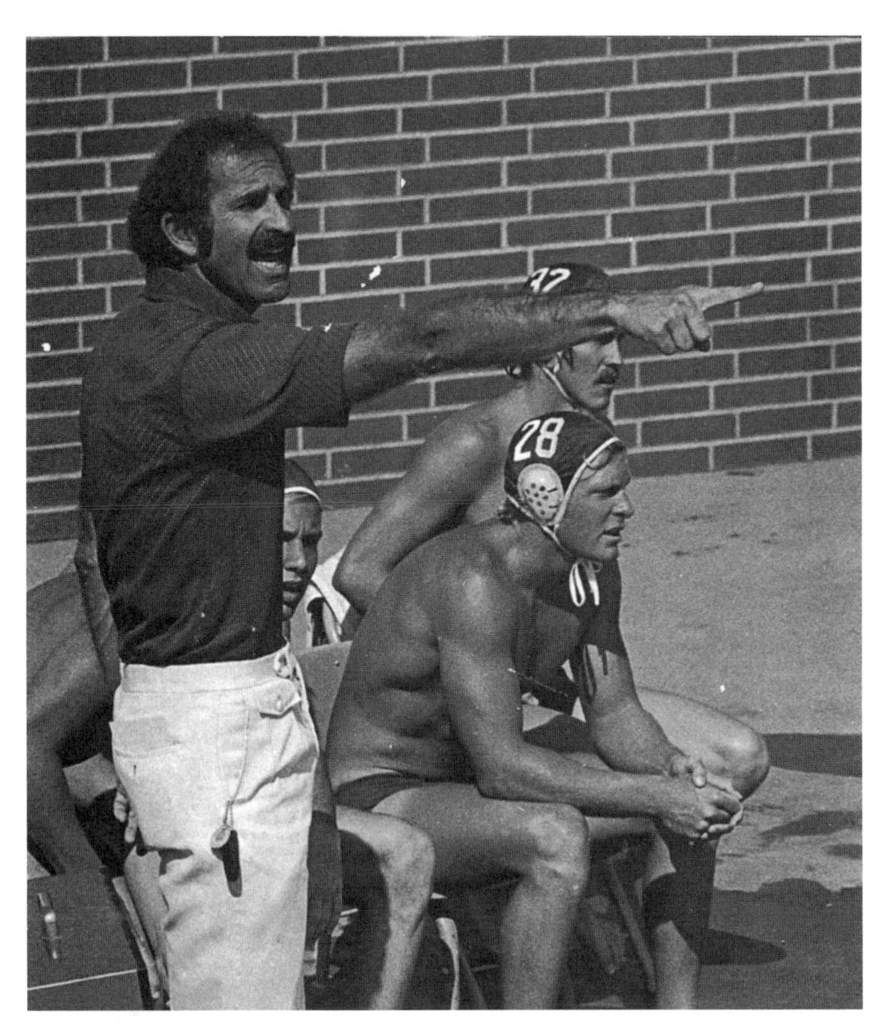

Too often, the healthy, life-affirming potentials of sports are submerged beneath a destructive performance principle. Instead, we should emphasize the pleasure principle in sports and exercise.

unity, thus supplanting the traditional body-as-object relation. To some degree, such experiences promote better understanding of how it feels to live within a culturally conditioned male body—a body generally severed from its consciousness and treated as an implement in the world of work.

The traditional male mind-body split has been characterized as both alienating and objectifying. This form of psychical-biological organization is evident in many social behaviors. Feminists have been outraged by men's tendency to regard women as sexual objects rather than persons. Heterosexual and homosexual rape are male crimes, whereas cases of sexual assault by women are very rare (Kanowitz 1969, 18). Males are also vastly more prone than females to commit crimes of violence (Simon 1975). Boxers and football players are trained to deny their own pain, yet they are expected to hurt or cripple their opponents. The great daredevils who risk life and limb for fame have been mostly male. Warfare, almost always a male preserve, entails the risk of one's own physical being as well as the denial of the enemy's right to life. Genocide has been almost exclusively a male activity. Dehumanizing institutions such as slavery and the early factory system were initiated and justified by men of power.

To imply that these social behaviors and institutions are outgrowths of an inherently male mind-body relation would be reductionistic. Nevertheless, the available evidence indicates that a restructuring of male consciousness and the male mind-body relation is a prerequisite to the evolution of full sexual equality.

REFERENCES

Boadella, David. 1974. *Wilhelm Reich: The Evolution of His Work*. Chicago: Henry Regnery.

Fisher, Seymour. 1974. *Body Consciousness*. New York: Jason Aronson.

Kanowitz, Leo. 1969. *Women and the Law*. Albuquerque: University of New Mexico Press.

Reich, Wilhelm. 1972. *Character Analysis*. New York: Farrar, Straus and Giroux.

Simon, Rita James. 1975. *Women and Crime*. Lexington, Mass: Lexington Books.

Jocks in the Men's Movement?

MIKE MESSNER

Since the late 1960s, the left/counterculture has denounced organized competitive sports because of the Lombardian ethic that "winning is everything." The emphasis on goal-oriented competition, many have argued, fosters alienation from oneself and others, and reinforces the most destructive elements of a racist, classist, and sexist society. In the 1970s, the emerging profeminist men's movement added a more personal dimension to this indictment of sports by revealing that many boys and men in sports experience pain, anxiety, loneliness, insecurity, and failure.

In short, critics viewed sports as a threat to a healthy self-image, as a barrier to intimacy between men, and as an impediment to building an egalitarian, cooperative community. Out of this rejection of organized sports has come what Jack Scott (1972) called the "countercultural ethic": "New Games" should emphasize universal participation (instead of a "star system"), the importance of the process over that of the goal, and a loose spontaneity instead of a rigid rule structure. Essentially, the counterculture and the men's movement have sought to replace "sports" with "play."

This rejection of sports by the men's movement is rooted in a very valid critique of our society and in the truly bad experiences many boys and men have had with sports. But a small and growing number of men within the men's movement are beginning to view this outright rejection of sports as both a hindrance in attracting "mainstream men" to the movement and as a problem for men already in the movement.

For better or for worse, a vast number of men in this society strongly identify with the sports world. In focusing on the negative and ignoring the positive things that men get out of sports, we in the men's movement can only further alienate ourselves from mainstream men. As a tiny and hardly influential movement, we should recognize that sports could serve as a major point of intervention in working with men to develop a critique of masculinity. Sports is the only part of life in which many men experience fun with other men, where they push their bodies toward excellence, where they learn to cooperate toward a shared goal, and where they find a sense of community in an increasingly alienating and privatized society.

The second problem with the men's movement's outright rejection of sports is that there are, in fact, a number of "closet jocks" in the movement who have often felt defensive and guilty about their continued interest in sports. There has been no opportunity within the movement for them to discuss their experiences in sports as a legitimate part of their lives. In speaking with these "men's movement jocks," I have found they share common experiences. In response both to their own bad experiences as athletes and to the countercultural critique of sports, many of these men rejected sports outright in the 1970s. But in so doing they felt a sense of loss. Now some of these men are reapproaching sports—often cautiously—and even attempting to reclaim sports as a valid part of their lives. But this time they have a very different attitude, and a different perspective on what it means to play or to watch competitive sports. Cooper Thompson, whom I interviewed at the 1983 National Conference on Men and Masculinity, is representative of the emerging "men's movement jocks."

FROM RACING TO RUNNING

Cooper Thompson is a thirty-four-year-old man who lives in Boston. He has worked as a teacher in alternative schools, and he is currently training teachers in New England to incorporate nonsexist content and practice into their teaching. He is very active in the national antisexist men's movement.

From a very early age, Thompson was pressured to be a "success," both in school and in sports. He always felt that he was in a sort of race with other men to prove himself. And he was truly successful by all external standards: he was a good wrestler and an all-league football player in high school. He was well liked by teachers and coaches and was given a prestigious "student-athlete" award. And he had "lots of dates" with girls. But behind the glow of success was a feeling of unease, unhappiness, and loneliness.

During Thompson's college years at Brown he was "very lonely." He played some hockey but stopped playing most sports, and as a result his weight increased from 160 to 190 pounds. After college, he rejected the "very competitive Eastern environment" he had grown up in. He got involved in noncompetitive physical activities such as hiking, climbing, and cycling, and for the first time in his life he began to feel good about himself. In 1975 he moved to Colorado to help start a new alternative school. During his three years there, he "began to develop an understanding of sexism, sex role stereotyping, and started to use that stuff in school." Interestingly, he was awakened to the reality of "sex-role stereotypes" through an athletic experience with a female colleague at the school, who was a "real strong feminist."

> The turning point in my relationship with her and in my understanding of feminism was the day when Molly and I decided to teach a class in rock climbing. So we said, fine, why don't we go out and do some climbing just to check ourselves out. So I'm assuming that I'm a

> better climber than Molly and that I'm stronger than her—and we get to these rocks, and we're climbing up, and I start to get a sense that she's a little bit better climber than I am. And we go up to the top, make this move, and *I can't make the move!* She's gone up ahead of me and protected it, and I can't make it up there! And that just sort of broke through some stuff in my relationship with her, and we began to communicate about the fact that I had been putting her down a lot and assuming she wasn't very competent, and assuming I was better than her. And then I began to learn a lot from her about feminism and the way women are treated by men, and that really made a difference to me.

After moving back to Boston in 1981, Thompson started running, partly as a way of dealing with the stress associated with the move, his unclear occupational status, and a difficult relationship. After watching the Boston Marathon, he decided to train to run in it. In his first marathon, his friend Paul helped him deal with his nervousness, fear, and physical pain in the last few miles. Now, he's "addicted to marathons." He explains,

> There's something really wonderful about running with other people and having a sense that we're all in it together—knowing I want a good time, but having no illusions about being one of the top finishers—and I never will be.

Thompson still feels a sense of competition when he runs, though:

> There is some sense of wanting to beat other runners, but I know I have no chance to win. I think there are limits to how fast I can run, given my age and given my general body structure. The whole race was just so enjoyable and

Cooper Thompson: "I want running to be an enjoyable, friendly activity and at the same time a challenge."

> I became clear that I want running to be an enjoyable, friendly activity and at the same time a challenge.

At the age of thirty-four, Cooper Thompson now appears to be developing a more comfortable sense of who he is in the world. He knew that the "traditional male competitive role" did not make him happy—even when he was "successful" at it—and he is working personally, professionally, and politically to change the destructive aspects of traditional masculinity. But he still enjoys competitive sports. Perhaps his earlier focus on traditional male success left him feeling unhappy and empty because it prevented him from experiencing the intimacy with other people that he craved. And perhaps having now begun to overcome some of the barriers to intimacy that were imposed upon him by rigid definitions of masculinity, he can now approach sports and competition in a more balanced way. He's getting back into playing basketball, and he likes an "intense" game. He likes to "play hard," but he also wants to appreciate those whom he plays with as people. In trying to balance the "traditional" definitions of masculinity and sports with the "emerging" ones, he admits to sometimes feeling a bit confused and ambivalent:

> I guess I sometimes feel like it isn't OK to be a real jock and to be really competitive, so I'm a little apologetic about it. But, on the other hand, I only want to be competitive if no one else gets hurt. I really do want to play basketball in a way that is very loving with other people. When I'm really supportive of other players is when I'm having the most fun—when I really don't care who wins or loses.
>
> In terms of the men's movement, I don't think I've talked to anyone else about this in the men's movement. There's a lot of negative images about sports there. But I got a real sense of the nurturant potential of sports this fall when I was running with my friend Paul, and I said to

myself, "There's something about running with another man, about being with other men in athletic events that I actually love and that I don't get being with women." See, Paul and I grew up very athletically with a lot of competitive stuff, and we have kind of an unspoken thing about what it means to compete, and what it means to sort of push ourselves through some soreness and some aches and pains—not complaining, just sort of pushing—that's just wonderful. There's some kind of spirit about running with a man next to me, knowing we're both tired and we're pushing each other, and we don't say anything about that. And we're also good friends—so when we reach across during the time when we're running and hold hands, or stop and hug each other at the end, there's something about that spirit that I just really love. And I don't want to feel apologetic about that.

FEMINIST ANALYSIS OF MEN IN SPORTS

DON SABO

In November 1986 I was invited to make a keynote address to the First Multidisciplinary Conference in Sport Sciences, in Lillehammer, Norway, on the ties between patriarchy, men, and sports. In attendance were about two hundred scholars, researchers, coaches, and sports physicians from Scandinavia, Western Europe, and North America. My chief goal was to demonstrate that feminist perspectives are useful for understanding men's lives.

From a feminist perspective, we can see that sports bear many elements of patriarchal social organization, norms, and ideology. Further, we recognize that a main function of traditional sports is to teach conformity to patriarchal values. Some men may wonder why their needs are not met in relationships with other people, why they gravitate toward violence, or why they feel as though they are fending off a possible attack or failure. From a feminist viewpoint, socially structured sexual inequality is largely responsible for leading men down these alleys. Traditional sports are an important part of this process.

Feminist analysis helps reveal how sports, especially contact sports, train boys and men to assume macho characteristics like cut-throat competitiveness, domination of others, tendency toward violence, emotional stoicism, and arrogance toward women. Feminist analysis also highlights how social structures affect men's lives. Sexual inequality in sports, it shows us, not only gives more athletic opportunities to males than females, but sport's intermale dominance hierarchy—the "pecking order" that jocks know so well—pits man against man, enabling the few men in powerful positions to exploit the dreams and control the actions of those under them. In the end, males are separated from women and set against one another.

The nexus between manhood and patriarchy in sports is a good place to begin raising critical questions and men's consciousness. In the 1960s, the feminist critique of the housewife-mother—a cluster of roles and attitudes that so many women had assumed—stimulated much insightful writing and discussion among women. A feminist critique of men's sports has a similar potential for important insights, because the athletic experience is so personally intense and socially pivotal for many males, whether they are jocks, fans, or anti-jocks. Since sports and masculinity have been strongly associated in American culture, and since most athletic organizations are male-only, an analysis of sports can also foster knowledge of how men and their institutions work.

Men who are trying to analyze the "male experience" from the feminist paradigm are often misunderstood by other men, who tend to equate feminist analysis with women's studies, and to assume that only women can take part in that. Many men feel that sex inequality and sexism are women's problems, not men's.

Women are also often wary of men who apply a feminist analysis, for a different but quite understandable reason. They worry that men who have begun to research and write about gender and masculinity ("men's studies") will take over women's studies programs, in which women are numerous and wield some power. Nonetheless, although women have made great progress exposing and analyzing inequality between men and women, few feminist thinkers have recognized that the social structure of gender relations also involves a system of intermale dominance, in which a minority of elite men dominates the masses of men. Each of these patterns of domination feeds on the other; like sex roles, they are reciprocal. By analyzing the male pecking order in sports, we may better understand the larger processes of sexual inequality.

So my main goal in Norway was to entice men to think like feminists, and to invite women to expand the purview of feminist analysis to include the study of men, masculinity, and intermale dominance. My speech encouraged sports researchers to think about the old association between men and sports in new, feminist ways. Feminist theories are no more the property of one sex than other innovations in scientific thought. The feminist paradigm, with its unique concepts, methods, and assumptions about its subject matter, allows both sexes to rethink all aspects of human existence. Feminist visions have the potential to help men recognize and escape from their own oppression as well as to challenge the position of women in the capitalist patriarchy.

LESSONS OF LOVE

I learned an important lesson in Norway. Meeting so many active and healthy athletes and coaches, and bathing in the energy and optimism that permeates much of athletics, reminded me how much I really love sports despite its dark side. The truth is that sports are both a joy and an affliction. Many of the lessons athletes learn through sports—to set and pursue goals, to seek excellence, to listen to and care for their own bodies, accept loss as well as victory, to work with others against the odds—are worthwhile for people young and old. Likewise, some elements of traditional masculinity are worth saving and instilling in our children.

The historical significance of the Norwegian conference became dramatically evident to me when I noticed a huge oak desk in the lobby of the Lillehammer Hotel. I wondered why the desk was not being used for anything other than supporting an oversized flower-filled vase. I discovered that the desk is actually a symbol of the Norwegian people's

The widespread emergence of powerful, competent women athletes challenges men to rethink our assumptions about the supposed "natural" differences and inequalities between men and women.

liberation from the Nazi occupation during World War II. Once used by a German commandant during the war, the desk later served for the signing of Germany's letter of surrender.

Immediately after learning about the desk, I went to a talk on male sexuality and nineteenth-century sports given by Todd Crosset of Dartmouth College. Nineteenth-century sports, he argued, helped define male sexuality as distinct and superior to female sexuality. I realized that here was a man in 1986 earnestly discussing sexism and male sexuality from a feminist perspective when, in the same conference room some four decades earlier, black-booted Nazis paraded their ideology of domination. Hope and energy welled up inside me. I do not believe, as Freud and others would have it, that the sons are destined to repeat the sins of the fathers. Feminist perspectives can be useful in helping men reconsider and redefine manhood and society in ways that ensure, rather than erode, our capability for love and survival.

MEN'S RESPONSES TO WOMEN'S MOVEMENTS

Someone once said that the fish are the last ones to discover the ocean. And so it is with men and patriarchy. Despite patriarchy's longevity and strength, men have failed to reckon with the fundamental realities of social grouping by sex. For more than a century, however, feminists have challenged men and women to look critically at gender issues and eliminate some of the injustices that attend sex inequality. Lately, men are beginning to listen. Many men seem intimidated by feminists and other women who do not play traditionally feminine roles. Some men act afraid of the changes they think that feminism represents; some react with anger and hostility.

Other men, though, have taken the feminist challenge to redress inequality and seriously rethink gender issues. A critical dialogue about men and masculinity has emerged during the past ten to fifteen years. It is critical in that it sees men and masculinity as a problem. It recognizes that there is something rotten in the ways that manhood has been defined, the ways that men spend their lives, and the ways that men relate to one another, to women, and the planet. Increasingly, men are beginning to reconsider their identities, their sexuality, and the violence they have shown toward women and toward one another. A new area of writing and research, men's studies, not only seeks to critique men's lives, but to help men change themselves and reweave the latticework of their relationships with women and with one another.

When I was a college student in the early 1970s, I was dissatisfied with many of the gender games I felt obligated to play out with my male friends and women. I just never felt comfortable with the traditional male role—acting confident and cool with women when I felt insecure and vulnerable, being tough on the outside and never talking about the personal issues that churned on the inside. I didn't realize it at the time, but I was searching for alternatives to the old masculine role. I wanted a "new suit of clothes," so to speak, that I felt more comfortable wearing in daily life. I discovered there were women on campus who also felt constrained and inhibited by the traditional gender roles. Most of them considered themselves feminists. I began to seek out their company. I read feminist books and attended women's lectures. The discovery of feminists and feminisms helped me to reconsider and rebuild my life and gender identity.

As a man interested in feminism during the early 1970s, I felt rather alone and a bit weird. There were not thousands of men signing up to join the women's movement! Eventually, however, more men began writing and talking about gender issues. Men's support groups began to sprout up, and the new men's studies literature gave me more to read and think about. A profeminist men's movement emerged, and I got involved.During the 1980s, the men's movement grew. Today, tens of thousands of men not only support gender equality but are committed to forging more healthful, humane, and nonsexist ways of being men. The followers of Robert Bly's "mythopoetic men's movement" use chants and drumming to help men get in touch with what are said to be the cultural roots of masculinity. The National Organization for Men Against Sexism (NOMAS) struggles against sexism and explores gender issues as varied as men's violence against women, men and spirituality, reproductive rights, men's health, men and pornography, homophobia, bisexuality, and gay rights. Some organizations advocate for fathers' rights. Religious denominations have begun sponsoring weekend retreats and support groups for men.

SEEKING PERSONAL AND SOCIAL CHANGE

One of the most powerful lessons I learned from feminism is that "the personal is political." This means, among other things, that we should not view our personal lives as totally separate from events in society, politics, or history. It means that we can better understand our own gender identity by exploring the social and historical contexts in which gender identity emerges, and vice versa. Many men in the men's movement stress the importance of exploring the inner roots of their masculinity and, in the process, of transforming their identities. They're doing this important psychological work in support groups, in men's conferences, at men's weekend retreats, and in counseling. Other members of the men's movement emphasize the need for men to ally themselves with women to secure pay equity in the workplace, better access to good child care, an end to domestic violence and rape, and a more peaceful society.

Both these approaches to change are necessary. Yes, we need personal change, but without changing the political, economic, and cultural structures that surround us, the insights forged within individuals will fade away. Personal change needs the support of institutional change. Without a raft or boat or some structure to hang on to, even the best swimmer will tire and slip beneath the waves.

Boys and Girls Together: The Promise and Limitations of Equal Opportunity in Sports

MIKE MESSNER

When I was in grammar school in the late 1950s and early 1960s, the best athlete in my classes never got to play with us. She was a girl. Somehow we boys all knew that Debra could run faster and hit a baseball farther than any of us, yet we never had to confront this reality directly. Our teachers, by enforcing strict sexual segregation on the playground, protected our fragile male egos from the embarrassment and humiliation that presumably would have resulted from our losing to a girl. In that pre-feminist era, insulated within the all-male world of athletics, our attitudes and values about the "natural" differences between males and females developed and solidified unchallenged. Athletic girls such as Debra were rare. At best, they were shunted aside and ignored; at worst, they were ridiculed and dismissed as "sex deviants."

Largely because of the women's movement, sports sociologists and historians have recently begun to reconsider the meaning of sports as a social institution. Clearly, a major role of sports in the twentieth century has been to provide an institutional context for "masculinity validation" in a rapidly changing world. The prominence of sports—in schools, on television, in conversations, and so on—can be largely attributed to the fact that sports are a male-created, homosocial subculture that provides dramatic "proof" of the "natural superiority" of men over women.

In modern times, the experience of playing (and watching) sports has been, for boys, an important part of the socialization process into manhood. Boys learn through sports to place great value on competition and winning, to "take" physical pain and "control" their emotions, to view aggression and violence as legitimate means to achieve one's goals, to accept uncritically authority and hierarchy, and to devalue women as well as any "feminine" qualities in males. In short, organized sports have been a school of patriarchy for boys. But what happens when girls and women begin to move into organized sports in great numbers, as they have in recent years? What will be the effect on boys, on girls, and on the overall system of gender difference and inequality in society?

THE UPSIDE: CHALLENGING SEXISM AT ITS ROOTS

There has been a great deal of controversy about "cross-sex competition" in recent years. Although little comprehensive research has yet been done on this issue, one reasonable hypothesis is that having boys and girls compete together from an early age will help break down sexist stereotypes. Since there are no significant physiological differences between males and females throughout the elementary school years, we can expect that girls, when given truly equal opportunities and encouragement, will be able to compete as equals with boys. Sociologist Janet Lever's research (1976) suggests that cross-sex competition among children could help girls develop the self-confidence and attitudes that may enhance their roles as adults in public life.

Having girls and boys play organized games and sports together can help challenge outmoded gender stereotypes, and lay the groundwork for the development of mutual respect and equality between women and men.

But what effect will girls' movement into sports have on the socialization of boys? Consider the following recent anecdote: an eight-year-old boy on a playground proudly told me, "My best friend is the best basketball player in my whole school." Only incidentally did he mention to me that his best friend is a girl.

Systematic research will give us a better idea of whether or not girls' movement into sports will have a dramatic impact on gender socialization, but this boy's attitude suggests that he and his schoolmates are accepting a reality from which I and my male peers in the fifties and sixties were insulated: girls *can* be good at sports; perhaps they can be just as good or even better than boys. Letting boys face this fact during childhood, when their attitudes are being formed, could lead them to more easily accept women as equals in adulthood.

THE DOWNSIDE: THE LIMITS OF EQUAL OPPORTUNITY

Before concluding that females' participation in sports is an unambiguously positive change that will undermine sexism, we should examine two important concerns.

First, many people believe that equal opportunity within the present sports world will "socialize" girls to the values that are helpful for achieving "success" in public life as adults. Sports may well teach values, but these values are not unambiguously good. Despite the common belief that sports build character, there is little evidence that athletic participation has made males happier, healthier, or more successful. My research with former athletes suggests that extreme adherence to the athletic role actually serves to exacerbate the most destructive elements of traditional masculine identity. In particular, the extreme goal-directedness that the successful athlete adopts tends to undermine his ability to establish and maintain intimate relationships with women and with other men. Given this, it is as yet unclear whether women's movement into sports will lead to the humanization of men and sports or to the dehumanization of women.

A second, related point is that simply giving girls and women equal opportunity in sports will not necessarily completely change sports' role in the perpetuation of sexist ideology. Although equal opportunity in elementary school sports can contribute to the shaping of more egalitarian attitudes among children, we must recognize that, from adolescence on, male and female bodies tend, on average, to differ in size, strength, endurance, muscle-fat ratios, and so on. And since succeeding in the "money sports"—football, basketball, hockey, etc.—requires attaining the most extreme possibilities of the male body, it is unlikely that females will ever be able to compete equally with males in the higher levels of these sports.

This fact is crucial to the ideological role that sports play in gender relations. Consider, for instance, what one middle-aged man told me: "A woman can do the same job I can do—maybe even be my boss. But I'll be *damned* if she can go on the football field and take a hit from Ronnie Lott!" That this man (and perhaps 99 percent of all U.S. males) probably could not take a "hit" from the likes of pro-football player Ronnie Lott and live to tell about it is irrelevant, because football has symbolic meaning for men. Football gives individual men the opportunity to identify—abstractly and generically—with all men as a superior and separate case. In contrast to the semi-bare, vulnerable bodies of the cheerleaders on the sidelines, the armored male bodies of the football players testify that, at least on the football field, men are clearly superior to women.

Women do have some physical advantages over men that could be translated into athletic superiority. For instance, a different skeletal structure and greater body limberness make for superior performances on the balance beam. But most women competing with men in any of the more highly valued sports would be at a decided disadvantage. With women competing on a male-defined turf, the sports media could employ statistics, "objective measures of performance," to show incontrovertible evidence of the "natural" superiority of males over females. And male sports announcers and reporters could simply smile and shrug: "We just call 'em as we see 'em."

Granting boys and girls equal opportunity to play sports will help undermine the sexist ideology that reinforces gender inequities in society. But recreation supervisors, teachers, coaches, and parents should realize that simply giving girls equal opportunity with boys may ultimately do neither girls nor boys a great favor. It is crucial that we also examine the underlying value system of organized sports. Otherwise, we may simply be attempting to hammer females into an institution that does not work all that well even for most males. Equal opportunity is a lofty and reasonable goal, but we should ask ourselves, equal opportunity to do *what*?

REFERENCE

Lever, Janet. 1976. "See Differences in the Games Children Play." *Social Problems* 23, 478-87.

Different Stakes: Men's Pursuit of Gender Equity in Sports

DON SABO

I was returning home from the 1993 Women's Sports Foundation annual conference when the last leg of my flight was delayed by thunderstorms over La Guardia Airport. After being grounded for two hours, the passengers turned to one another for conversation and diversion. Two young men near me, having overheard me talking about women's sports, asked whether it is true that women's athletic programs benefit from the money that men's football programs generate. I explained that this idea is basically a myth; according to records maintained by the National Collegiate Athletic Association (NCAA), about 87 percent of all football programs (45 percent of NCAA Division I-A football teams and 94 percent of Division I-AA football teams) lose money (Raiborn 1990). Rather than being the goose that lays the golden egg, most big-time football programs siphon money away from women's athletic programs as well as lesser-status men's athletic programs.

In response to my comments, the young men explained that their intercollegiate sports (fencing and track and field) "are also getting screwed by the athletic department, which is only interested in promoting football." The fencer lamented that "the women athletes have Title Six, or whatever it is, to help them fight for better treatment, but the guys in the smaller sports don't have anything working for us. Nobody is out there pitching for our interests."

"Hold your horses, guys," I retorted. "First of all, it's Title Nine not "Six," and it may be more in your interest to support it than you might suspect."

I explained that Title IX was enacted by Congress in 1972 to stop discrimination on the basis of sex in any program or activity receiving federal financial assistance. The male-dominated intercollegiate athletics establishment fought against the implementation of Title IX through a multimillion-dollar lobbying campaign during the 1970s. The forces against sex equity in sports won legal support in 1984 with the Grove City v. Bell case, which limited Title IX's ban on sexual discrimination to specific programs, rather than entire institutions, that receive federal funds. However, Congress put the legal bite back into Title IX with the passage of the Civil Rights Restoration Act in 1988. Since then, the legal and social forces seeking gender equity in sports have been getting stronger. I encouraged the two athletes to learn more about Title IX, because nondiscriminatory athletics will not only benefit female athletes, but most male athletes as well.

THE GUISES OF SEXISM IN SPORTS

The struggle for Title IX in athletics is a struggle against sexism. Sexist ideology has taken on many guises in the history and development of modern sports. In the nineteenth century and in much of the twentieth century, sexism helped men to keep women out of sports. Since men's aggression, strength, and competitiveness were believed to be biologically based, athletics seemed a natural activity for boys. Notions about women's physical frailty, emotional passivity, and nurturing proclivities helped keep sports an exclusively male domain. In this early phase of sports history, therefore, sexism served mainly to reinforce sex segregation.

Later, particularly after the 1972 passage of Title IX, sex segregation in sports began to break down. Women's rapid development of their athletic skills chipped away at timeworn stereotypes of femininity and masculinity. Between the late 1960s and early 1980s, the number of women participating in college sports increased between 300 and 500 percent (Guttman 1991; Johnson and Frey 1985). Ironically, however, at the same time women were joining sport teams, men were taking over the coaching and leadership positions in women's sports. Whereas more than 90 percent of women's coaches were women before passage of Title IX, fewer than 50 percent of coaching jobs are held by women today. And women now hold fewer than one-third of the administrative positions in women's college athletics (Acosta and Carpenter 1993). The net professional result for women can be described as increased perspiration without political representation.

For the past twenty years or so, sexism has served in sports as an elitist ideology that helps men to control the female athletes, coaches, and administrators who now occupy the corridors of what many men still consider a male domain. Elitist sexism assumes that men perform better in athletics than women do, that traditional male approaches to competition ought to be emulated by the female newcomers, and that the largest share of human and fiscal resources are best spent on men's games and men's health rather than women's games and women's health.

We seem to be entering a new era, though—one in which sexism is taking the form of a wounded giant. Sexist remarks are usually unspoken, and the guardians of the patriarchal status quo no longer call for the exclusion of women from athletics. There is hardly any public rhetoric, in fact, about preserving traditional masculinity or femininity. Instead, opponents of gender equity say it will lead to the deterioration of competitive standards and the erosion of athletic excellence. Woeful predictions are made about sagging support from alumni and dwindling university public relations. Gender equity is equated with organizational detumescence. Behind such assertions is the assumption that the existing male-dominated system for organizing and defining

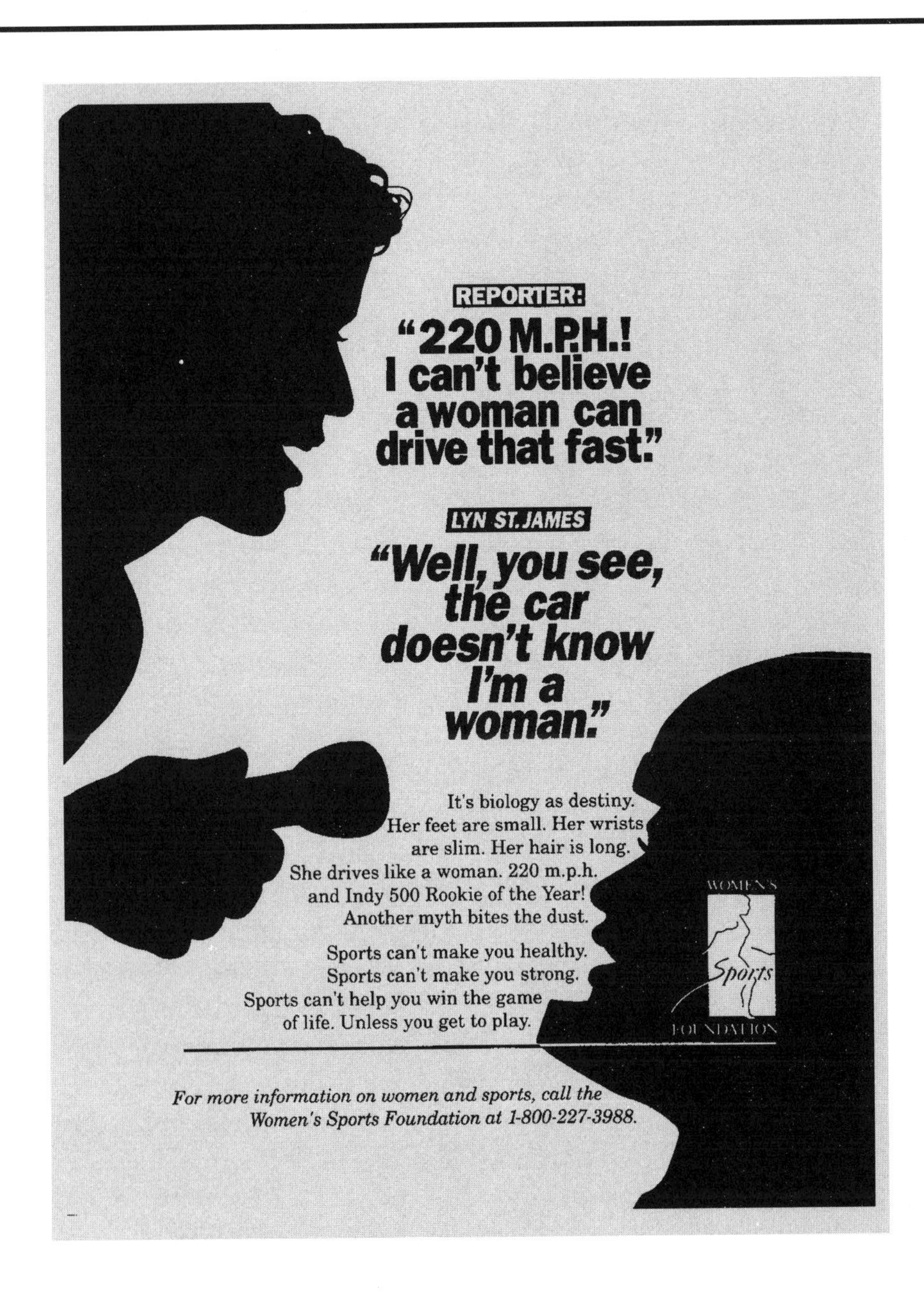
REPORTER:
"220 M.P.H.! I can't believe a woman can drive that fast."
LYN ST. JAMES
"Well, you see, the car doesn't know I'm a woman."
It's biology as destiny.
Her feet are small. Her wrists are slim. Her hair is long.
She drives like a woman. 220 m.p.h. and Indy 500 Rookie of the Year!
Another myth bites the dust.
Sports can't make you healthy.
Sports can't make you strong.
Sports can't help you win the game of life. Unless you get to play.
WOMEN'S Sports FOUNDATION
For more information on women and sports, call the Women's Sports Foundation at 1-800-227-3988.

sports is, after all, best for everybody. To support gender equity, therefore, is to oppose sports. No one wants to do that, so the institutionalized inequalities in elitist, male-dominated sports remain in place.

Wounded-giant sexism is divisive. Besides pitting men against women, it pits heterosexuals against homosexuals. Have you ever wondered why you don't often read about or hear whispers about gay men in sports although you may hear a lot of rumors about lesbian athletes? It's not became there are no gay men in the locker room. It's because homophobia isn't being used to discredit and beat down men's sports the way it is being used against women's sports. Wounded-giant sexism also pits coaches and administrators of elite men's sports against coaches and administrators of women's sports and less prestigious men's sports. My contacts in NCAA circles tell me that the gender-equity issue is increasingly being framed as a struggle between so-called revenue-producing sports and lesser men's sports. The opponents of gender equity are trying to divide and conquer.

Wounded-giant sexism also isolates and marginalizes those male coaches and male administrators who lean toward adoption of more educational, inclusive, and equitable athletics. Some men are paying a high personal and professional price for their activism on behalf of gender equity in athletics. Rudy Suwara, a former volleyball coach at San Diego State University, claims he was fired for insisting on equal treatment for female athletes. Jim Huffman, a coach at California State University at Fullerton, has filed a lawsuit alleging that, because he assisted his women's team in regaining the varsity status that was stripped away from them, he was not retained when the department restored the team. I regard these men as unsung heroes. Just as white men in the civil-rights movement learned there are knocks to be taken for advocating racial equality, men who have allied with the forces of gender equity have faced the political heat. Guts, vision, and commitment can help douse the flames.

And, finally, the key assumption behind wounded-giant sexism—that the system has enough troubles already and that more reform will wreck all of sports—defuses the efforts of racial and ethnic minorities to promote change. The message carried from the captains above to the deckhands below is don't rock the boat—and it makes no difference whether the hands on the oars are women's hands, black hands, brown hands, yellow hands, or red hands.

Whether in its separatist, elitist, or wounded-giant form, sexism benefits the elite men who sit atop the administrative hierarchies that were formed in the historical heyday of patriarchal sport. In the 1990s, sexism is thwarting the efforts of less advantaged groups in sports to transform athletics into a more equitable, democratic, and healthful institution.

MEN ARE DISCOVERING TITLE IX

The Women's Sports Foundation (WSF) operates as a clearinghouse for information about women's sports and fitness. WSF also promotes greater opportunity for girls and women in athletics, from the grass-roots level through school programs, Olympic sports, and professional sports. In over ten years of work with WSF, I've witnessed growing interest from men in achieving gender equity in sports. In the early 1980s, few men fought for the rights of female athletes. Today, however, more men are waking up to the fact that gender equity is their issue as well as women's. More men are beginning to realize that they have different stakes in the institution of sports than their dads or older brothers did in the male-dominated past. Men are not only gaining knowledge about Title IX and gender equity, they are acting on it as well. Many are organizing to get a fair shake for the girls in their schools and communities. Some are pursuing lawsuits on behalf of daughters, teams, or clients. Following are some examples, mostly from WSF files, of men's efforts to pursue equal opportunities for girls in sports.

- A maintenance man from Buffalo, New York, felt it was unfair that the local high school did not offer as many athletic programs for his daughters as it did for his sons. He gathered basic information about Title IX, composed a letter stating his concerns, and, along with several other parents, petitioned the school board for changes in policy.

- A male school board member got funding for a sex-equity evaluation of his Oregon school district. The evaluation saved the girls' field hockey team from dissolution and prompted improvements in the schedules for girls' sports events and in the girls' locker-room facilities.
- For the past three years, the members of the men's wrestling and rugby teams at a northeastern university have helped women to organize a recognition and awards breakfast in honor of National Girls and Women in Sports Day. Along with the women, they plan, decorate, sell tickets, wait on tables, and clap and cheer.
- When David Chapman, a mortgage loan officer and volunteer basketball coach from Dallas, Texas, first saw his nine-year-old daughter's gym, he was shocked by its poor condition. There were no bleachers, the flooring was worn linoleum tile, and the lighting was inadequate. The boys' gym, he discovered, was modern and well equipped. He joined forces with other parents, brought media attention to the inequities, and helped to teach the school board about matters pertaining to Title IX (Shuster 1993).
- A basketball coach in a southeastern Division II college is working with an attorney to redress apparent sex-based discrimination in the granting of athletic scholarships.
- The father of a soccer player approached a Western school board about creating a girls' soccer team at his daughter's school. A survey of students revealed high interest in girls' soccer, yet the board voted down the request. The father has hired an attorney.

Katherine Reith, the assistant executive director of the WSF, says that men can promote gender equity in athletics by being more aware of sexism in the sports pages. Men can phone or write newspaper and magazine editors, she suggests, to ask for more coverage of women's sports, or to complain about sports journalists who praise women's beauty rather than their athletic skills and accomplishments. She encourages men to show support for girls' and women's sports by attending games and events. Men can also donate funds to women's programs. When making a contribution to a former high school or college athletics department or alumni association, men might request that the funds be routed to women's athletics.

Finally, men can resist sexism in the locker room. Whether it's in the fitness center, the men's shower, a love relationship, or the workplace, personal behavior says a lot about gender politics. Men can quit going along with the tits-and-asses remarks that demean and devalue women. Men can question comments that belittle women's athletic abilities and accomplishments. I recall watching the "regulars" playing basketball one day at the YMCA to which I belong. A tall, strong woman had joined the usually all-male lunchtime pickup game. She definitely knew her way around the court. Later, when the guys filed into the men's locker room sweating and puffing, I asked them what they thought of her play. A lawyer quickly replied, "She didn't have nice tits." Rather than laughing or remaining silent, I pushed him a bit: "Give me a break, Bill. Don't hand me that sexist bullshit. You know she was right in there with you guys." He then admitted that she played better than "a lot of guys can," and the guys talked for five minutes about how far women had come in basketball during the past ten years. This may seem like a small step to take in the face of the formidable foe of sexism, but, in my mind and heart, I sense that as long as we men allow stereotypes of femininity to go unchallenged, we will remain saddled with masculine stereotypes as well.

MEN'S STAKE IN GENDER EQUITY

Friedrich Nietzsche announced in the nineteenth century that God is dead. Nietzsche did not mean that spirituality had ceased to exist or that God had keeled over with a brain aneurysm. Rather, Nietzsche was observing that the traditional relationships between Western people and their God had been transformed by modernity. He recognized that the timeworn cultural representations of God didn't suit modern realities.

At the dawn of the twenty-first century, I am suggesting that masculinity is dead. Men's relationships to the icons of traditional masculinity have been transformed. The Marlboro man succumbed to lung cancer. Rock Hudson turned out to be gay. On some campuses, fraternity "brothers" are getting our daughters drunk and gang-raping them. Even Superman is six feet under the ground. Indeed, there is no one "masculinity" in American culture; there are only masculinities. Men are finding diverse ways to construct and explore their gender identities and personal relationships. Fewer and fewer men are protecting images of manhood that no longer fit the realities of their lives. They are slowly realizing that the old norms for manhood just aren't cutting it in the postmodern marriage and family, in the workplace, in government, or in sports. Traditional masculinity has become an imitation without an original (Butler 1989).

We're dealing with what sociologists call "cultural lag," which means that our conscious minds haven't caught up with changes in institutional realities. For example, the industrialization of American society had transformed the day-to-day relationships between the sexes, in marriage, family, and the workplace, long before feminists began to criticize patriarchy and reconsider what it means to be a woman or a man, a wife or a husband, a mother or a father. Feminist analyses of culture were, to a large extent, responses to institutional changes that had already occurred. Feminist politics and critiques also spurred social and political trends toward egalitarianism. In the same way, the old cultural equation of sports with masculinity no longer reflects the realities of sports in the 1990s. Women are no longer "entering" sports; they're already here. Women have already challenged the old patriarchal definitions of sports and competition. Men are changing, too. Mariah Burton Nelson, in her book, Are We Winning Yet? (1991), observes that some men are helping to shape a "partnership model" in athletics that mixes cooperative values with competitive practices, strengthens the healthy body rather than putting it at risk for injury, and promotes respect and caring for teammates and opponents. Many female athletes and unknown numbers of their male counterparts are embracing this model and moving away from the traditional "military model" in athletes, in which sports are regimented, hierarchical, highly competitive struggles designed to facilitate domination and subjugation of others.

Increasingly, men are recognizing that the military model just doesn't work for them. For me, twelve years of football led to seven years of lower back pain and a major surgery. I'm not alone. There is an invisible army of former athletes, now in their forties, fifties, and sixties, who deal with the pain and anguish of injured shoulders, knees, backs, and hips. There are the overworked coaches who've gained coronary thrombosis or broken families in exchange for winning records. There are guilt-ridden men who made injured athletes play so they themselves could win games, save jobs, or earn promotions. There are the millions of men and women who opted out of athletics by age fourteen or fifteen. Can you imagine creating and defending business practices that alienate 75-80 percent of your long-term customers? Think of the thousands of would-be coaches and administrators that would be working with these kids today if they had not been processed out of the elitist, hypercompetitive athletic model.

Finally, a growing number of antisexist men not only support gender equity but side with women on issues such as men's violence against women, sexual harassment of women in the workplace, and the sexual abuse of women by male coaches. Some male coaches of women athletes use sexual tension or power to control their athletes. Male coaches need to look long and deep into their gender identities and sexualities and come up with answers to these problems. Indeed, within the military model of sport, traditional coaches rarely empower their athletes. Coaches arrange for the election of "captains" and extol the virtues of team leadership but, in the end, the coaches make all the decisions. Literally and figuratively, the coaches "call all the shots." The Marine Corps doesn't really build men as much as it manufactures conformists. Is there a parallel here with traditional coaching?

In summary, sexism is not a woman's problem or a man's problem. It is a social problem. It is a sports problem. Today much of the athletic experience is distorted or muted by sexist ideologies that hinder personal efforts to grow and change.

Whether separatist, elitist, or taking the guise of a wounded giant, sexism is gnawing away at the gut and soul of sports. Sexism belies the fundamental athletic ideal that everyone should become all that she or he is capable of being. In the 1990s, exposing sexism wherever it exists, and fighting gender equity, will prove to be part of the cure for modern sports, not part of the illness.

Football continues to be the main roadblock stalling reform efforts in intercollegiate sports. Ideologically, football epitomizes traditional masculinity and the military model in athletics. Football is also a major structural obstacle to reform. By providing many full-time scholarships, most college football teams commandeer exorbitant funds without returning profits on their investments. As Todd Crosset, a sports sociologist and a pro-equity NCAA swimming coach, has said, "What football scholarships are to athletics, nuclear arms are to the Cold War." The Berlin Wall has fallen, but efforts to scale back munitions production have been persistently opposed. Similarly, Title IX was passed more than twenty years ago, and yet the not-so-wounded giant of male-dominated sports lumbers forward. In the end, lesser-status men's sports as well as women's sports are being shortchanged.

Gender politics in sports no longer fit into the "we-men versus they-women" pattern. Indeed, complex politics of masculinities are operating in athletics. Many men who make their livings from sports continue to fight to maintain the male-dominated status quo. They are angered or frightened by the threat of gender equity in sports. As one athletic director put it, "Everything I have worked for has been deemed unjust, and it's very, very hard for me to accept." A male coach confided, "I support the idea of equity, but I also have to live and work with guys who are not exactly in love with the idea of handing over more resources to the women." Other men, though, are struggling for gender equity in athletics because they feel it means fairness and a better life for them, the girls and women in their lives, and their institutions and communities. They are learning that the struggle to implement Title IX can be a vehicle for constructing modes of manliness that reach beyond sexism.

Today the stakes for changing sports and masculinity are higher than ever, and fewer men are betting on the patriarchal past. They are not betting at all. They are busy envisioning and creating more equitable futures.

REFERENCES

Acosta, R. Vivian, and Linda Jean Carpenter. 1993. "Women in Intercollegiate Sports: A Longitudinal Study—Fifteen Year Update, 1977-1992." Brooklyn, New York: Brooklyn College Department of Physical Education.

Butler, Judith. 1989. *Gender Trouble: Feminism and the Subversion of Identity*. New York: Routledge.

Carpenter, Linda Jean. 1985. "The Impact of Title IX on Women's Intercollegiate Sports." In *Government and Sport*, ed. Arthur T. Johnson and James H. Frey, 62-78. Totowa, NJ: Rowman and Allanheld.

Guttman, Alan. 1991. *Women's Sports: A History*. New York: Columbia University Press.

Raiborn, Mitchell. 1990. "Revenues and Expenses of Intercollegiate Athletics Programs." Overland Park, KS: National Collegiate Athletic Association.

Changing Men through Changing Sports: An Eleven-Point Strategy

DON SABO AND MIKE MESSNER

The 1990s loom large with potential for rethinking and changing gender relations and sports. We have identified some strategies our readers might use to help change the traditional relationships between sports and masculinity. Our ideas are intended to help you change the ways you think about sports and the ways you participate in athletics and exercise.

1. Be a Buddy to Your Body: Resist definitions of masculinity that put bodies at risk, glorify pain, and promote or ignore injury. Develop athletic potential in ways that are challenging but not physically harmful. Renounce painful and risky training practices. Confront and report instances of verbal or physical abuse of players by coaches. Reject locker-room clichés that encourage athletes to disregard the limits and vulnerability of their bodies, such as "No pain, no gain," and "You gotta pay the price to win."

2. Stop Excessive Violence in Athletics: Change the rules and challenge the underlying values of games that promote violence and excessive aggression. Developing less aggressive forms of sports will make them safer for athletes and erode harmful cultural equations between sports, masculinity, and violence.

3. Recognize Men's Issues in Sports: Identify men's issues in sports. Profeminist men have advocated an end to rape, domestic violence, sexual abuse, and sex discrimination in the workplace, and other forms of oppression of women by men. Yet we have been very slow to recognize that men also oppress other men. Why is it that profeminist men can immediately recognize the injustice of a man beating his wife, yet muster only a vague criticism of two men beating the pulp out of each other in a boxing ring?

4. Resist Locker-Room Sexism: Refuse to laugh at sexist jokes in the locker room. Challenge your friends when they ridicule women or treat them as sex objects. Don't let bullies get away with intimidating younger or weaker boys. Confront them face to face, or get help from coaches, athletic administrators, or school officials.

5. Fight Sexism in Sport Media: Do not tolerate sexism in sports media. Phone or write television or radio stations that promote sexist stereotypes—female athletes as sex objects, or male athletes as "dumb jocks." Insist that newspapers provide equal coverage for women's and men's sports. Boycott companies that use sexist images of male or female athletes to market their products.

6. Teach Young Athletes Non-Sexist Values and Practices: Parents, coaches, P.E. teachers, and community groups can teach children to recognize and question gender stereotypes in sports, such as in comments like these: "Sports are for boys," "Jane is good at baseball because she's a tomboy," "You throw like a girl," "This game wasn't made for sissies," or "He hits like a pussy." Work with young people to redefine sports values and practices. Provide children with opportunities to participate in a wide range of competitive and cooperative athletic experiences.

7. Work for Gender Equity in Athletics: Seek to develop gender equity in youth sport programs, high school sports, and intercollegiate athletics. Get to know your school athletic programs. Help make the fundamental principle of gender equity a visible, dynamic, and ongoing dimension of program planning and evaluation. Embrace the educational ideal expressed by the *Final Report of the Knight Foundation, Commission on Intercollegiate Athletics* (March, 1993) (7, 8):

> The equity issue transcends athletics politics because it goes to the heart of what higher education is all about. Colleges and universities advance their intellectual mission by placing a premium on fairness, equality, competition and recognition of merit. These values are as important in the department of athletics as they are in the office of the dean. Keeping faith with student-athletes means keeping faith with women as well as men. The goal to keep in mind is the imperative to create comparable opportunities for participants, whether men or women, while controlling costs.

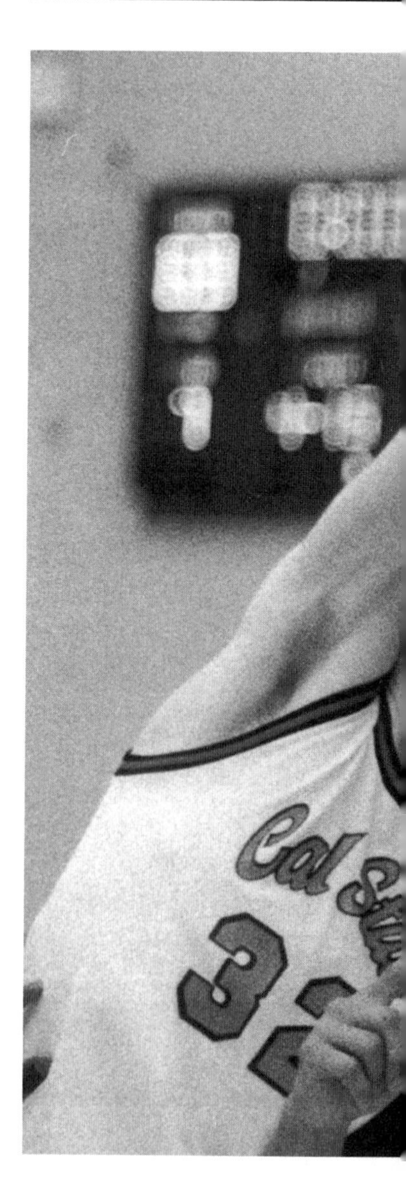

Before the potential of sports to contribute to healthy bodies, friendships and communities can be fully realized, the racism, sexism, and homophobia that are currently built into the sports establishment must be directly confronted.

8. Confront Homophobia and Heterosexism in Sports: Recognize that homophobia and heterosexism are forms of prejudice. Support educational efforts that aim to eliminate homophobia in sports, and support moves by gay and lesbian athletes to "come out," and new athletic institutions such as the Gay Games.

9. Become an Advocate for Minority-Group Athletes: Help people of color avoid exploitation in sports. While urban schools deteriorate and inner-city jobs become more scarce, hundreds of thousands of African-American and Latino youth continue to see sports as a ticket out of the ghetto. For the vast majority, though, sports are a round-trip ticket back to the ghetto. Insist that schools and community organizations link the athletic activities and dreams of minority-group youth to solid educational agendas. Develop ways to use sport as a tool for raising the educational aspirations and achievements of minority-group youth.

10. Get More Women Involved in Sports: Work to maximize women's participation in coaching and athletic administration. Greater numbers of women in athletic leadership positions will provide girls with more role models to look up to. Male athletes will also benefit from increased opportunities to observe and work with women in non-traditional roles. Stereotypes of masculinity and femininity, especially as they have been promulgated in sports, will break down with more female leaders. Mutual respect and cooperation between the sexes in athletics will be encouraged. And including more women of color in sports leadership positions will promote understanding and respect for racial and ethnic group members.

11. Push the "Man Question": Men need to be more assertive about taking on the "man question" in feminist theory. In the past, men have sometimes felt like intruders in women's studies circles. There is an important difference, however, between interloping on the professional opportunities of female academics (who *already* face formidable sex discrimination) and tapping the feminist paradigm for inspiration and guidance.

SELECTED READINGS ON MEN, GENDER, AND SPORTS

Cohen, Greta L. 1993. *Women in Sport: Issues and Controversies*. Newbury Park, CA: Sage Publications.

Curry, Timothy J. 1991. "Fraternal Bonding in the Locker Room: A Profeminist Analysis of Talk about Competition and Women." *Sociology of Sport Journal* 8:119-35.

Fine, Gary Alan. 1987. *With the Boys: Little League Baseball and Preadolescent Culture*. Chicago: University of Chicago Press.

Funk, Russ Ervin. 1993. *Stopping Rape: A Challenge for Men*. Philadelphia: New Society Publishers.

Griffen, Pat, and Charmaine Wijeyesinghe. 1992. *Homophobia on Campus: A Workshop*. Pelham, MA: Diversity Works.

Kidd, Bruce. 1987. "Sports and Masculinity." In *Beyond Patriarchy: Essays by Men on Pleasure, Power, and Change*, ed. M. Kaufman. Toronto and New York: Oxford University Press.

Klein, Alan. 1993. *Little Big Men: Bodybuilding Subculture and Gender Construction*. Albany, NY: State University of New York Press.

Kopay, David, and Perry Dean Young. 1977. *The David Kopay Story*. New York: Arbor House.

Lenskyj, Helen. 1986. *Out of Bounds: Women, Sport and Sexuality*. Toronto: The Women's Press.

Majors, Richard, and Janet Mancini Billson. 1992. *Cool Pose: The Dilemmas of Black Manhood in America*. New York: Lexington Books.

Meggyesy, Dave. 1970. *Out of Their League*. Berkeley: Ramparts Press.

Melnick, Merrill. 1992. "Male Athletes and Sexual Assault." *Journal of Physical Education, Recreation and Dance*, May-June: 32-5.

Messner, Michael A. 1992. *Power at Play: Sports and the Problem of Masculinity*. Boston: Beacon Press.

Messner, Michael A., and Donald F. Sabo, eds. 1990. *Sport, Men and the Gender Order: Critical Feminist Perspectives*. Champaign, IL: Human Kinetics.

Nelson, Mariah Burton. 1991. *Are We Winning Yet? How Women Are Changing Sports and Sports Are Changing Women*. New York: Random House.

Nelson, Mariah Burton. 1994. *The Stronger Women Get, The More Men Love Football: Sex and Sport in America*. New York: Harcourt Brace and Company.

Pronger, Brian. 1990. *The Arena of Masculinity: Sports, Homosexuality, and the Meaning of Sex*. New York: St. Martin's Press.

Sabo, Donald F., and Ross Runfola, eds. 1980. *Jock: Sports and Male Identity*. Englewood Cliffs, NJ: Prentice-Hall.

RESOURCES AND ORGANIZATIONS

Athletes for Sexual Responsibility and Rape Awareness. For information on the videotape "Rape Awareness," write Dr. Sandra Caron, 5749 Merrill Hall, Room 15, University of Maine, Orono, Maine 04469.

Changing Men. Magazine. P.O. Box 908, Madison, Wisconsin 53701.

EMERGE. A counseling service for men who batter. 18 Hurley Street, #23, Cambridge, Massachusetts 02141.

Federation of Gay Games. 584 Castro Street, Suite 343, San Francisco, California 94114.

Mentors in Violence Program. A student athletes' project aimed at increasing rape awareness and reducing sexual violence against women. Northeastern University's Center for the Study of Sport in Society, 360 Huntington Avenue, Suite 161 CP, Boston, Massachusetts 02115.

National Organization for Men Against Sexism (NOMAS). Suite 300, 54 Mint Street, San Francisco, California 94103.

Men's Anti-Rape Resource Center (MARC). P.O. Box 73559, Washington, D.C. 20056.

Real Men. An anti-sexist men's group committed to public education and political action. P.O. Box 1769, Brookline, Massachusetts 02146. 617-782-7838.

Women's Sports Foundation. Eisenhower Park, East Meadow, New York 11554. 800-227-3988.

ABOUT THE AUTHORS

Mike Messner holds a Ph.D. in Sociology from the University of California at Berkeley. Presently, he is an Associate Professor in the Dept. of Sociology and the program for The Study of Women and Men in Society at the University of Southern California in Los Angeles. He is the author of *Power at Play: Sports and the Problem of Masculinity*. A former high school and college athlete, he has two sons.

Don Sabo holds a doctorate degree in Sociology. He is a Professor of Social Science at D'Youville College in Buffalo, New York. He is the co-author of *Jock: Sports and Male Identity, Humanism in Sociology* and *Sport, Men, and the Gender Order: Critical Feminist Perspectives.* He recently addressed the U.S. Olympic Committee's National Coaching Symposium in Colorado Springs. He is a parent, a fitness enthusiast, and a former NCAA Division I defensive football captain.